She Holds the Face of the World

10 Years of VoiceCatcher

Tiah Lindner Raphael - Managing Editor
Nancy Flynn - Poetry Editor
Judith Pulman - Prose Editor

Introduction by Liz Prato

©2015 VoiceCatcher
Authors hold the rights to their individual works.
All rights reserved.

Original Artwork incorporated in Cover Design:
   "A Series of Events" ©2013, Sarah Fagan

Book Layout & Cover Design by Shawn Aveningo, The Poetry Box®

Introduction by Liz Prato

Managing Editor: Tiah Lindner Raphael
Poetry Editor: Nancy Flynn
Prose Editor: Judith Pulman
Copyeditor: Helen Sinoradzki
Editorial Assistant: Meghana Mysore

Printed in the United States of America.

No part of this book may be reproduced
in any matter whatsoever without written
permission from the author or publisher except in the case
of brief quotations embodied in critical essays,
reviews and articles.

ISBN-13: 978-0-692-49793-7
ISBN-10: 0-692-49793-5

Published by VoiceCatcher, 2015
Portland, Oregon
www.VoiceCatcher.org
info@VoiceCatcher.org

She Holds the Face of the World

Dedicated to the founding members
of the VoiceCatcher Editorial Collective

Thanks to these six visionaries,
the voices of hundreds of women
have been celebrated and shared
over the last ten years:

Marti Brooks
Diane English
Sara Guest
Jennifer Lalime
Elizabeth Jones
Emily Trinkaus

Contents

Foreword ~*Tiah Lindner Raphael* xi
Introduction ~*Liz Prato* 1

Poetry

From the Poetry Editor ~*Nancy Flynn*

    Our Singular Women's Lives 6
    Voices: Caught 7

One

    Advice ~*Donna Prinzmetal* 9
    nichos: woman at the window ~*Jodie Marion* 10
    The Moth, the Last Night ~*Amy Minato* 11
    The Amateur Tomato Breeder Flirts ~*Jennifer Lesh Fleck* 12
    For a Hot Shot ~*Susan DeFreitas* 14
    Two Poets in the Weight Room ~*Tricia Knoll* 15
    Rendezvous ~*Rebecca Starks* 16
    Thicker Than Water ~*Claudia F. Savage* 17
    Weddings I Have Ruined ~*Tanya Jarvik* 19
    Swan Song ~*Jaime R. Wood* 20

Two

    Osprey Circles ~*Tiel Aisha Ansari* 22
    Birdsongs in Traffic ~*Naomi Fast* 23
    I didn't keep it a secret, I just didn't tell you ~*Celina Wigle* 24
    Three Facts about Sperm ~*Ursula Whitcher* 25
    After Finding Out My Sister's Pregnancy Is Not
        ~*Shanna Germain* 26
    We ~*Carrie Padian* 27

Mama Takes a Bubble Bath ~*Kristin Berger* 28
Guilt Poem: Conflict ~*Brittney Corrigan* 29
Jailhouse Call ~*Kelly Running* 32
Motherhood ~*Elizabeth Stoessl* 33

Three

Portrait of a Cowboy as a Young Girl ~*Carolyn Martin* 36
The Old Life ~*Andrea Hollander* 37
Waiting for a Diagnosis ~*Linda Strever* 38
315C ~*Kristin Roedell* 39
Binders Full of Women ~*Shawn Aveningo* 41
The Figurehead ~*Darlene Pagán* 42
Aurelia Aurita: Moon Jelly ~*Lois Rosen* 43
Starfish Time ~*Jodie Buller* 45

Four

Under the sign of the water bearer ~*Jennifer Kemnitz* 48
Polaroid of My Mother ~*Cindy Stewart-Rinier* 49
Still Life with Cabbage ~*Margaret Chula* 50
The Hand-Off ~*Pattie Palmer-Baker* 51
Three Rings at the Same Time and Performing Tigers
 ~*Victoria Wyttenberg* 53
Said & Meant II ~*Meredith Stewart* 56
Violet at the Creation ~*Wendy Willis* 58
The Hundred Names of Love ~*Annie Lighthart* 59

Five

Unexpected Conversation at Mid-Life ~*Dawn Thompson* 61
To Those Boarding Planes to Hawaii to Escape the Rain
 ~*Judy Beaudette* 63
On the Book ~*Oz Hopkins Koglin* 64
How Can You Live There? ~*Bette Lynch Husted* 65
Some Shelter ~*Kate Gray* 66

city spacious heart ~*Pearl Waldorf* 67
spoon ~*Brandi Katherine Herrera* 68
Trucker's Atlas ~*Favor Ellis* 72

Six

Morning ~*Miriam Feder* 75
Pump House ~*Marj Hogan* 76
Anticipation ~*Penelope Scambly Schott* 77
Decomposition ~*Pat Phillips West* 78
Caring for Father ~*Heidi Schulman Greenwald* 79
'A'ā ~*Burky Achilles* 80
Bridge ~*Jennifer Liberts* 82
Tango Club—Valparaiso ~*Alice Hardesty* 83

Seven

More Like Music ~*Sage Cohen* 85
The Fujita Scale ~*Toni Partington* 86
To the Friend Who Talked Me Down ~*Amy Schutzer* 88
Relic ~*Jennifer Foreman* 89
Sleep ~*Emily Kendal Frey* 90
A Passing Music ~*Barbara LaMorticella* 91
Solder ~*Paulann Petersen* 92
Talking Herself into Onward ~*Melanie Green* 93

Prose

From the Prose Editor ~*Judith Pulman*

Twenty-Two Stories about Us 96

One

Robins ~*Jill Elliott* 99
Stoop ~*Jennifer Springsteen* 105
Forget about Florence Nightingale ~*Patricia Kullberg* 107

Kali-Ma ~*Amanda Sledz* 118
How I Learned to Rap in Jail ~*Susan Russell* 120
Wisdom Tree ~*Julie Rogers* 130
Running with Dragons ~*Trista Cornelius* 135

Two

Carnage ~*Heidi Beierle* 139
Left As It Was, It Would Come Apart ~*Jackie Shannon Hollis* 142
Your Hand at Your Throat ~*Karen Guth* 147
Dying to Get Out of Here ~*M* 149
This Morning ~*Susan Dobrof* 156
Black Sharpie ~*Anne Gudger* 158
30 Degrees from the Horizon ~*Cara Holman*. 166
The Bösendorfer ~*Alida Thacher* 167

Three

Tribes ~*Thea Constantine* 176
Messages ~*Mary Mandeville* 180
Vulvar Fantasy ~*Nikki Schulak* 187
Ablaze ~*Heather Durham* 195
Quality Courts ~*Patty Somlo* 197
Like Water and Stones ~*B.E. Scully* 204
Gene Kelly at the Door ~*Liza Langrall* 212

Acknowledgments 215

Contributors 223

Index of Contributing Writers 241

About VoiceCatcher 245

Foreword

When Diane English conceived the dream that would become VoiceCatcher, it came to her as many great ideas often do: with quiet footsteps in the back hallway of the mind.

The first glimpse came through a poem written about "women who hear the cries of the world. Women who catch the joy and the pain, the rhythm and music in voices of all kinds." The dream further revealed itself through serendipitous connections and conversations that eventually brought together the first editorial collective. VoiceCatcher was born.

Over the years, VoiceCatcher has grown, sometimes gracefully and sometimes awkwardly, as all newborn creatures must do. Leaders have come and gone. The journal has evolved. There have been successes and joys, but also false starts and reassessments. However throughout this change, VoiceCatcher has remained true to the voices from that first dream.

The magic that happens in our—your—organization is often a quiet magic. It isn't always something that happens on the pages of the newly-released journal, in the excitement of a reading, in the nominations for anthologies. The miracle that is VoiceCatcher happens when a woman speaks her truth through her art, when one woman reaches out to another with words of support and friendship, when someone who thought she'd never find a home finds her place in the warmth of our creative community. The real work of VoiceCatcher happens every day in the cycle of birth and rebirth that is the act of creation.

So while we celebrate our first decade as an organization with in-person events and this beautiful—no, stunning—volume in your hands, don't forget to see VoiceCatcher in the small moments in your own life. When you get up to write or paint or draw at 4 a.m. because of the quiet dream in the back hallways of your mind, honor that impulse to breathe life into the void. That is VoiceCatcher. When you reach out to another woman in support of her art, you're a part of VoiceCatcher. Together we are creating and recreating this living, breathing organization over and over through our acts of solidarity and love.

Diane's original dream echoes in us all and will continue for many more years. Thank you for joining with your sisters in the beauty of this journey.

Tiah Lindner Raphael
Managing Editor

Introduction

In 2005, a group of women set out to create a community that connects, inspires and empowers women writers and artists in the greater Portland and Vancouver area. Their dream was named VoiceCatcher. A large component of their vision included providing a publishing medium—first in print, and now online—exclusively for women. I've always been a big proponent of "If you want to change the world, start in your own backyard," and VoiceCatcher has done just that—and will continue to, for years to come.

Why, in the twenty-first century, do we need a venue dedicated to publishing the work of women? Because, it turns out, the twenty-first century is still somewhat in the Dark Ages when it comes to gender parity in publishing. In 2010, VIDA: Women in the Literary Arts released its first ground-breaking "Count," a survey of the top literary magazines' records on publishing male and female writers in the previous year. Women had long been expressing dismay and anger at the gender bias—unconscious or otherwise—they experience in publishing, but our concerns were often dismissed as unfounded and quite possibly paranoid. In response, VIDA decided to examine and publish the empirical evidence.

The first Count was a relatively small sample in terms of the number of publications reviewed, but they surveyed the most prestigious publications in the country: the journals, presses and anthologies that define success in American literature. Their findings speak for themselves: of the *New York Times* 100 Notable Books of 2009, 68 were authored by men, and 32 by women. The *Washington Post*'s Best of 2009 included 126 books by men, and 44 by women (one was co-authored by a man and a woman). *Publisher's Weekly*, the industry bible, listed 71 books by men, and 29 by women as the best of the 2009; more alarmingly, of their Top 10 Books of 2009, all ten were authored by men.

The proof was right there, in the numbers. Yet many criticized the limited scope of The Count. VIDA didn't shrink away; they continued to expand it to include more publications, as well as an historical count of prestigious book awards and prizes, some going as far back as 1901 (The Nobel Prize for Literature: 94 male winners v. 13 women as of 2013). Some members of the larger writing community continued to grumble about the efficacy of The Count, but others stood up and took note. They recognized they were, at best, falling short of gender parity in publishing and might need to examine their unconscious bias.

The most recent count of 2014 shows some publications made great strides towards gender parity, while others (pssst, *Harper's*! 144 men to 69 women) continued to reinforce the unacceptable status quo.

In order to combat the bias, it's important to understand the root of it. Women's writing and art have often been derided as reliant on the "personal"—relationships, sex, love, families and feelings and bodies. Serious, important topics—of war, politics and the economy, the principles on which civilizations are built and destroyed—are considered the province of male writers. A few women might boldly or blindly wander into the masculine territory, and critical attention is often focused on how successfully they did, or did not, cross the XY barrier. Damned if we do, damned if we don't. If we stay in the so-called "domestic sphere," we're considered quaint; venture onto a world stage, and we're treated like interlopers.

Roget's Thesaurus, Synonyms for Nonsense:

> baloney, rubbish, poppycock, bunk, baffle, flimflam, hogwash, hooey, and horsefeathers.

The women published by VoiceCatcher demonstrate unequivocally that the province of female writers *is* the world. No, wait—the universe. In this verdant volume of poems, stories and essays, local women have written about turtles and snakes and stars and limbs and smoke and flames and fuel. About back roads and dragons and faux rawhide and ghosts and ritualized rape. Orgasms and anger and sperm and blood, abortion, biopsies, addiction, violence and death. Breath.

VoiceCatcher's talented poets and prose writers detail the minute, but not the mundane. They turn their sharp lenses on the intimate details of our being—not just what it means to be a daughter, a sister, a wife, a mother, a friend and a lover—but what it means to be a sower and tender and gatherer of life on this earth. What it means to be made from the dust of exploding stars.

What else is there? What are wars fought over and economies built on and politics entangled with? Land and bodies. Our relationships with both. So when women writers are accused of focusing on the personal, I say *damn right* and *thank the goddesses*. The personal is everything, and without the female perspective, we would be lost.

VoiceCatcher is committed to continuing its mission of exposing the world through the lens of female writers and artists. The organization is a vehicle for change, for a better world. I hope you will join me in being a part of VoiceCatcher for years to come.

Liz Prato
September 2015

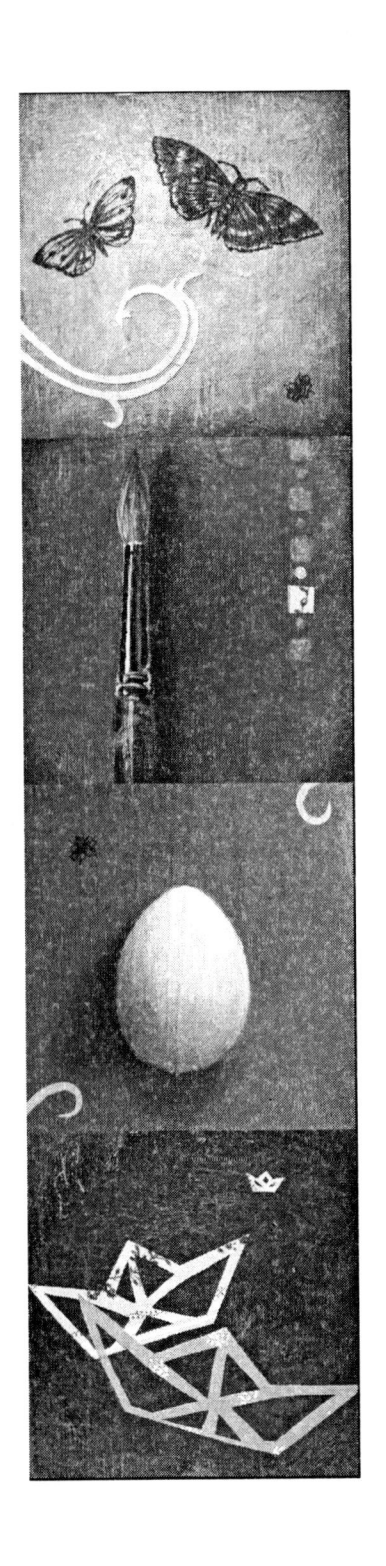

Poetry

From the Poetry Editor

Our Singular Women's Lives

Over ten years, and more than 300 poems whittled down to the voices of sixty women—that is what you have before you in the poetry section of *She Holds the Face of the World*. Poets from eclectic backgrounds writing poems about the cycle of life, rites of passage, our particular, singular women's lives. Included are not only the usual suspects so (still) worth talking about—love and family, birth and death, pitfalls and perseverance, aging and regrets—but also personal slants and new angles on subjects such as tomato breeding, tornado severity, and performing tigers.

Thank you to all of the women whose poems have graced the pages of *VoiceCatcher*'s print and online editions these past ten years. It was an *embarras de richesses*, to say the least, when our team of six readers divvied up this impressive body of work to tackle the challenging task of selecting which poems would be included in this celebratory anthology.

I wanted to write an introduction that would give you a sense of who these sixty women are and what their poems have been bringing to the world since 2006. I soon decided to let the poets tell their own stories, and in their own beautiful, heartbreaking, wise, and poetically inspiring words—

Nancy Flynn
Poetry Editor

Voices: Caught

> a found poem consisting of lines taken from
> each poem in the order in which it appears
> in She Holds the Face of the World

Today, before nightfall even, face the folds of deep. A candle laps yellow over new life, twisting a seed tucked between tongue and cheek. All stories are pulp, pumping up to dazzle. Reach, second nature, for a clean slate. No hillside will ever sigh at light too bright for pictures. Keeping time with the breeze, shadows criss-cross on the river's face. Here roots come through & unimaginable shapes unfold the other way to rush forward, a hollow curve of loss. One day I will stand up and say I know this wedge of water, slim parcel of time. Roll over, push that shadow out of bed. How I used to rock, cruised the highways, mugging for the camera. How almost easy it was to live even with disappointment. I want to divine a map, skirting the rain channeled by a mosaic whose mortar weakened year by year. The sunlight enters in threads and spots. Aren't we all water-filled animals taking in the shoreline upside down? At first, cajoling then push, the air escaping like a thousand exhalations no one would ever touch. Out the window, still purple, the mountain & fire going everywhere like water. You can't find what you don't already believe is there, something jeweled and unutterable, the hundred names of love. Fast, flurry, full. A small blue pond in the sky. Take the prescription, spreading wide to possibility. The words come flat like bottle caps perched at the edges & the wind is picking up. I taught myself how to sing on these roads. Awaken, spirit & speak! The whole of the valley in a whistling room, awaiting the moment when days shorten & sun sits low in the sky. One branch buried under earth. One perfect wave of understanding in that cold clear rippling water. For now, only the dance & leaning into the beat, a storm chaser who seeks the thrill. The knowable heart is an hourglass, speaking in tongues, fitted with arrows of what we know. Little mysterious sound on a summer day, streaks of sky darker than whatever mistakes they replace—stride on, forward the hope-gamble, muscle with faith.

One

Donna Prinzmetal

Advice

You can stop trying to be perfect right now,
today, before nightfall even.
Stand in the dizzying twilight
and count waves instead
each in-breath
each exhale.
There are things in this life you will not do:
fly, be a professional ballerina, learn Chinese
or soprano sax.
It's okay.
Open the hatch of your life and climb
into the unspoiled dark.
Wade in the thick marshes,
a turtle without a shell.
Collect agates. Be a pickpocket of your own dark past.
Try and find the right shade of yellow in the harvest moon.
Listen for owls.
Watch the crazy dance of bats.
Here we are,
each of us staggering through doorways
into other doorways.
Why are you always saying you're not ready?
None of us are ever ready.
Forgive yourself.
This will need to be done more than once
every single day.

Jodie Marion

nichos: woman at the window

at the open window
she imagines going
out, not down.

ancient eros-breed
of winged things,
she leaps

she folds herself
inward nine times,
a thick origami butterfly

shakes the weight
of *stupor mundi*,
cuts through the blue.

she holds the face
of the world steady, looks
long & deep into its glassy eye.

ॐ

open the glass inward.
steady the shaking eros.
imagine the leap.
face the folds of deep.
eye the down & out.
cut the wind's blue stupor.
look to the ancient,
winged world. fly.

The Moth, the Last Night

A candle laps yellow
over new life twisting
in its moon-lucent cocoon.

I move on your lap.
We watch the head burst skin first
laborious the breast. A pulpy body strains
through its stiff vest, heaving

a last leg loose.
The parchment skitters off.
Hunched, drying its cape of wings,
wet brown moth on wood table hovering.

Our own limbs loosen, we move apart.
A slow luminescence
of something born and lost.

Jennifer Lesh Fleck

The Amateur Tomato Breeder Flirts

Dumbed by the gloss of her lips,
his attraction hidden like a seed tucked
between tongue and cheek,
he can only talk about fruiting, staked vines
sweating in the Central Valley sun. Vanilla melts
into his cobbler. For twenty minutes he's held
the same spoonful as she bustles about, buses tables,

so he rambles on about fat worms
that squirm into his neat beds overnight,
minty monsters he must seek out, pluck
(Oh, the give of their soft bodies
pinched between forefinger and thumb!)
from leaves smelling greenly of tomatoes,
of pear and paste and steakhouse tomatoes,
a smell that reminds him it's early summer,
he could very well fall in love. And when

he confides in her that he sometimes flings
caterpillars against his garden wall, even enjoys
watching hornworms explode and streak
yellow pestilence, he likes that she smiles,
and doesn't blush, likes the bend
in her chubby legs when she laughs.

He goes on talking tomatoes,
thriving, succulent towers of fruit—
yellow Brandywine, Sungold,
Ruby Cluster, even the elusive
and strangely striped Green Zebra,
the one that never looks ripe, that keeps
its dapples till harvest comes. *When ready*,

he says, *the stripes sometimes blush pink.*

He leans hard against the counter, tells her this year
Cherries are her best bet. Hardy, easy to grow,
small and close to their wild forebears,
yet tight, plump, valued. And taken between lips
and teeth in the closest of kisses,
suddenly, explosively sweet.

Susan DeFreitas

For a Hot Shot

My words can't carry you
out of the smoke, the smoke
that took your lungs.
My words won't beat back the flames.
I can't remember when last
I provided anything
but fuel.

The heat is exhausting,
kindled by exhaust. A warning
in warming,
high in the wild blue
where maybe you
reside tonight
while your lady rains hot tears
on your black boots.

When will I stop trying
to revive you with wind, with prayer?

All stories are pulp.

All trees are fuel.

Tricia Knoll

Two Poets in the Weight Room

Verlena carries a black cane. I have lumpy veins.
Our ages add up to nearly a gross of years
in this hotbed of stair steps, ellipticals,
rowing machines, barbells, mirrors, and sweat.

Neither of us has stomach
for the maiming news on silenced TVs
or a captioned chef stuffing wieners
with cheddar cheese. I flaunt red
nails on heart-monitoring handlebars.
She wears a red sweatshirt. We show up.

I suggest we wait for the firefighters'
free gym access at eleven. They are cuter
than the upper-chest guy pumping up
to dazzle skinny boy learning squats.
Verlena lays down her cane, leans into
the upper-back torture rack.
She laments that no one guesses
she eyes groins and puffed-out pecs.

Doing lat pulls, I huff out how much I admire
tight-spanked butts when stuck in traffic, those men
in two-tone bike shorts zipping up the right lane,
the swervy audacity of steel-strung calves
on sculpted seats.

The firefighters never come. Something burns.
The two lifters trade hints on mixing slow counts
with heavy reps.

We flesh out odes. They count haiku.

Rebecca Starks

Rendezvous

It happened without me, a haiku. *Open the car door— / now the seat is occupied / with small pink petals.* They had to be more solid than my flesh. I'd parked under a row of cherry trees the week before they blossomed, and now this. I drove on through them, the old, daily route—falling all around me, *kamikaze*— and didn't flinch. My eyes closed to violence. It was only after I parked, at the top of the long hill, that my blindsight failed and I reached, second nature, for a clean slate. The raindrops gummed the wipers—petals rolled up flush between their fingers, swiping—*you can / Look now.* Trees around me dripped dry moss, fiddled new leaves against a lightly rosined sky. Mare's-tails, out of reach. Between us, reluctant metronomes folding up—*you stayed / away / so long.*

Claudia F. Savage

Thicker Than Water

He is not even here,
but the dinner conversation is going badly,
the guests are talking about some perceived evil:
oil and gas drilling, ranching, or pork
in such a way that the tone slants toward that place
where country people are only huddling,
dull-eyed sheep bleating for Jesus.

The guest who swirls her Cabernet is delicate in candlelight.
The guest who shivers, doubting the fact that I can shoot, compliments
my green beans. They are forking in the roasted potato, the room.
I want to show the guy my left hook
instead of the apple tart. This
I can stop.

Loving him muddied a line inside me.

I want to tell them, there is a woman in a wheelchair echoing
the blue hills' rain whether or not I am there to listen.
There is a cabin above the plum orchard
that you must stoop to enter. For 130 years
its planks let the world in. At dusk a bluebird's
call can carry through the blackberry to greet
the twilight.

There is his grandfather trying to save that
man falling into the cement pit, thick dust blinding.
There is his father pushing brooms through the
high school halls to fill his belly.
There is him, hiking into the mountains
in three feet of snow, gusts urging it below 20,
for so many hours that his fingers lose

their sense of touch and never regain it.
And how he didn't complain
as I wrapped blanket after blanket around him,
the skin on his knuckles elephantine,
cheeks furious with wind.

I want to tell them, no hillside will ever
sigh at your return. No pine sweeten.

His people never trusted me, and now,
have even less reason to,
still, he made his history mine.

He said this mountain will turn your legs to ghosts. These vines
are good for thickening. He lengthened his vowels
in the curve of my ear till they nested, sun-filled snakes.

Without him, I fear the clay rivers
will not recognize me. I fear there will be no welcoming
hillside, no leaf-tinged light. I fear I will be stuck
hearing Northeasterners chew their fattened beef
at my table forever.

Tanya Jarvik

Weddings I Have Ruined

by arriving with burrs in my socks,
gift in my dirty knapsack, pine cones rattling
in the box I wrapped with bad news

by saying how many pieces of toast
could have been spread with honey
for the price of your diamond ring

by being the one red dress in your lilac lineup,
those fat crayon scrawls in the guest book,
a wasp in your veil, a shrimp fork in your side

when I put orchids on wrong shoulders,
ordered light too bright for pictures,
toppled your cake, bared my gartered thigh

when I brought up the past, running late
but predetermined to make it in time
to shower congratulations on your future

when I rained, and rained, and rained
until roses, rice, confetti streamed away
leaving bride, groom, and guests marooned—

because you woke on that deserted aisle,
sea foam at your feet and catacombs in your hair,
cursing me for sailing home without you

Jaime R. Wood

Swan Song

      Whether the summer leaves waved
      in the wind, shushed and crackled
      as you walked into the woods,
      whether the pulse of crickets—
      their *threet-threet-threet* keeping time
      with the breeze—altered the pace
      of your breathing, whether you
      were stricken by the sounds
      of the forest, whether you saw the stars,
      paused as in prayer before you tucked
      the gun under your chin, or whether
      the clouds stared down like milky glass,
      makes a difference.

Two

Ciel Aisha Ansari

Osprey Circles

    Some days the ospreys hunt

                                    they only call

    the length of the river

                                  days when they soar

    back and forth

                                        for pure joy

    shadows criss-cross

                                  circles overlap

    on the river's face

                                  thermal air towers

                         framed by wings overhead

            chreeee

        chreeee

Naomi Fast

Birdsongs in Traffic

I can't help but look for the cracks
in every city. Here the sidewalk ends,
here roots come through.
I run from one end to the other
finding the river's edge
        insects in dead wood
birdsongs in traffic
        spider webs.
What is it I really want
if it's not the theater, the bars, the stadiums
a window over the river;
        if what I crave
is to be pricked by thorns
while clearing a place to plant?

Celina Wigle

I didn't keep it a secret, I just didn't tell you

when they told you
you would be sore for a while
they didn't mention
that the ache
would take on
unimaginable shapes
how it would quake
your stomach
six years in the future
when the young man above you
asked you
to have his children

Ursula Whitcher

Three Facts about Sperm

Sperm are like Chinese dragons:
they don't move straight.
They flick their tails around like unfolding a paper clip
then unfold the other way to rush forward.

Sperm are sensitive to calcium.
They don't stiffen like bone, they twist faster,
curl up on themselves like calligraphy practice.

Human sperm have it easy.
Frog sperm swirl through open water,
bleeding salt.

Shanna Germain

After Finding Out My Sister's Pregnancy Is Not

For six months, it seems she's swallowed
the moon bit-by-bit, hinge-jawed herself
open in hope of this new growth.

Skin shiny and rivered as washed-up stream stones,
body filling with light-caster, shape-shifter,
weight-bringer—it is hard to remember her shape before.

Grandma handles high weight and declares: girl.
We dig up baby names from memory's moss,
forget that some months the phases repeat.

Last quarter, her belly wanes crescent, empties
to a hollow curve of loss. Even shallow
arcs beneath her eye's hold nothing.

Calendar offers no new illumination.
I turn my face from the blue water pull of
my sister's eyes, hiding the half that knows:

It should have been me. Once, I carried my
regret so low if Grandma had seen,
she would have known better than try and name it.

In a dark place who knows what anyone
can see? I thought to be out of reach
of roots, arm buds, everyone else's future.

Greedy, hungry owl, I made a meal
of moon and spit it out, pelleted pile
of half-hearts and bones beneath the family tree.

Carrie Padian

We

I can't stop looking at these pictures of you
taking in every pixel
the play of light
and dark
the bend of brown around
your eyes staring
straight into mine
innocent
of the wanting
waiting there
memorizing
as if my knowing
means anything at all
as if one day I will stand up
and say I know
this face
better than anyone
and they will let me take you home with me
as if you have
no say
in the matter

Kristin Berger

Mama Takes a Bubble Bath

Wedge of water,
slim parcel of time,
her body traced by clouds
clotting and pulling apart,
a world adrift:
The porcelain suggests
that she lean back,
but how long legs reach,
this body of birth filling
every space water wants.

Mold in the cracks.
Smudges on eyeglasses.
Never perfect, nor nearly
enough. Here she rubs,
softens herself—pumice to heel,
cloth to nape—as if tuning
an instrument for what song
is expected next.

The children come
stand at the edge—
thousands of tiny bubbles explode—
the moment's metronome.
They try to comprehend
how she is
not on their side.

Brittney Corrigan

Guilt Poem: Conflict

When you tuck the blankets around
the hush of his body, turn off
the nightlight above his head, listen
to his even breathing and touch
your lips to his warm, sleep-red
cheek—this is when your guilt knocks
you back out of the room, presses
you down into your own bed,
and lies down beside you, whispering
all night to trouble your dreams.

You cannot believe you had the day
you had. Watching his lips part
in the darkened room, you cannot believe
this sweet, beautiful child was ever
anything else. You resolve that tomorrow
will be different. You will do better.
You will be patient and soft-spoken and kind.
You will count to ten, use your words,
keep your hands to yourself.

But morning comes with its assault
of noise and five-year-old limbs,
its torrent of contrariness and head butting,
sibling-strangling struggle.
You pry his fingers from your arms.
You wipe his spit from your face.
Carry him sideways under your arm
to the safe place behind his bedroom door.
You topple like a tower of blocks,
your alphabet unfamiliar, tumbling
from your mouth in some changeling
voice you don't want to accept as your own.

Love is not in question. You know
you would trade every minute of your life
for one of his—stand between him
and disaster, give him the last swig of water,
offer yourself in his place
to any stalking thing in the night.
But you have to say this.
You need to say this.
You know you can't be the only one.
The only parent who doesn't always enjoy
the company of your child. The only one
who dreads weekends and snow days,
who counts the minutes until bedtime, until
you can sit for one moment in a still house.

So when you kiss him goodnight, when
you lie down at last in a night-quiet room,
you force yourself to remember how today
he made up a new game and invited
you to play. Today, after the screaming,
the tears, the toys hurled at the closed
door, he sat on your lap and you rocked him
and nuzzled his every-which-way
hair. There were moments. And someday

he will be big. He will not need you
like this. His spindly, never-at-rest form
will no longer fit into your lap.
He will not remember
that these days left you broken.
Bouncing from time-out to spreading
out puzzles, to outside play,
he does not know this is hard.

It is you, not the child, who is lying awake
in the darkened room. You must
roll over, push that shadow out of bed,
and pitch it down the stairs. You must
remember that when the child wakes,
he always wakes singing.

Kelly Running

Jailhouse Call

The automated call from the jailhouse
coaxes me to answer, but
I disconnect from
the Russian roulette
of your life.

Press
'one' if you want to detox,
    'two' for a stint in rehab,
        'three' for the methadone that harbors a false sense of betterment,
            'four' for the black-tar street heroin,
                'five' for jail's gritty isolation.

A dealer hovers like a vulture
waiting for you, *Road Kill*,
my son,
and he will pick at your flesh
while you hold the dirty needle to your veins.

Sleeping tonight under a bridge,
will you remember how I used to rock you
as a baby,
singing a sweet melody of "Mockingbird"
to soothe your anxious cries?

Elizabeth Stoessl

Motherhood

Like no Cassatt or Morisot I've ever seen
(and what were those placid babies on anyway?
Did they suck in absinthe through their mothers' milk?)—
this canvas I view through visited windows:
A mother paces the alley behind her house,
and in a football-hold carries her infant girl,
the baby's angry head pointing
from her mother's elbow like a bullet
swaddled in tight fleece casing. As they march
the crunching gravel path the baby's screams
bounce off the sides of houses
into kitchens where neighbors
who've heard it and heard it for weeks
no longer rush to their windows.
Then finally—soothed by fall winds whirling
over a scalp red as her birthstone, now calming
to rosy pink—she defends her tiny eyes from the sun,
she closes them, and surrenders. She hushes.

I wonder if this peace could be achieved
by calmer means, more like those stoned
moms and babies in the paintings.
What wisdom do I have to offer this exhausted mother?
She knows how qualified I am: the one
who raised her child's father—putting him to sleep
face-down (to prevent a sudden death that we now know
my method could have caused),
coercing him to nap in a backseat cardboard box
as I cruised the highways. His unrestrained brother
once shook the box, sending the baby
sliding out and under the front seat,
to lie wedged, screaming, until the next exit.

Somehow, that baby survived my feckless ignorance
and sired this marvel of a girl, inheritor of his Olympian lungs,
the one to whom I surrender and hush.

Three

Carolyn Martin

Portrait of a Cowboy as a Young Girl

Mugging for the camera
in brand new cowboy boots,
she still insists she's Roy not Dale,
riding down the Happy Trail with Trigger
and the Sons of Pioneers.

She smooths her bronco-busting chaps,
pulls tight the fringe-cuffed gloves,
adjusts a broad brim hat that tilts
above her bangs straight-cut
and ties beneath a stubborn chin.

The lens clicks up the front porch steps,
corrals her closed-mouth smile,
her arms akimbo, stance girl-proud.
It's 1948. She's three,
decked out in faux rawhide.

This day, "You Are My Sunshine" plays
inside her head, the words exact,
a bit off-key. *You make me happy...*
those straight-on eyes convey... *please
don't take my sunshine away.*

I don't recall who shot this frame,
or how it felt to roam the Jersey shore
the King of Cowboys, Son of Pioneers.
I don't recall the guns, the fringe,
the voice that sang *when skies are gray.*

I can't recall when I was more
of me than on that sunless winter day.

Andrea Hollander

The Old Life

How almost easy it was to live
even with disappointment. If a boy
didn't phone or if he did and his voice was filled
with obligation, unmistakable as the residue
of flour left on my mother's breadboard,
I could bear it. And when suddenly only
other girls' bodies changed their lives
the way Cinderella's fairy godmother
transformed hers, though longing and envy
entered my own life, still it wasn't so difficult
to be patient. Downstairs in my mother's kitchen
I could count on the yeasty smell of dough
and my mother's experience in boy things.
Or there were dishes to do, a floor to be swept,
the pleasant necessity of usefulness.
If that didn't help, I could enter
my father's oak-lined study with its many books
and their soundless wisdom I believed echoed
my father's voice and his leather chair that echoed
the shape of his body. Sometimes I would sit there
in the quiet of that room as though I were already
a woman, wise and on my own, someone
experienced, who knew how to dole out
the particulars of justice to imaginary children
without altering my day's routine. How much better
my new life would be, how finally complete
and comfortable and on the other side of complication.

Linda Streuer

Waiting for a Diagnosis

for Lois

Three thousand miles away you fall
five times in two weeks, can't get up,
barely haul yourself out of a chair.
You're terrorized by an edge
of carpet, pebbles in the driveway.

I thought nothing but geography
would ever come between us. But now
you wander a singular wilderness. And I
want to divine a map, slog overland,
hack a trail, deliver you out of twisted
old growth and treacherous swamp.

Daylight hangs in precarious balance
as heavy clouds close against sun.
You like to say that when we met
my face shone like the moon, but I can't
give you even reflected light, can only
wait here, strike match after match,
trying to burn through all that dark.

Kristin Roedell

315C

The sign said *W LL W SPR GS*,
a nod to the muddy creek bed
where autumn leaves
floated like dead spiders,
bellies and legs to the moon.
It was the only hotel in town
that tolerated dogs—
with a pet deposit
management turned a blind eye
to its balding carpets.

At ten past, the street lights
cast parabolas
in the littered parking lot.
My daughter slept in the back
folded like an origami bloom,
dreaming dragons and fireflies.
Our collie had chewed through
the Mercedes floor mats
until bits of rug clung to her fur
like dandelion seeds.

There was a battered card stuck
to the office desk, tape curling:
HOURLY RATES, CASH ONLY.
My daughter yawned her way
into 315C, her hair matted
on the left side, skirting the rain
channeled by a broken gutter.
Boys slouched with hoods
pulled over ball caps,
and watched her.

Their cigarettes made scarlet
A's in the dark.

In the night, I counted the freckled
constellations on her back.
I thought long about what leads women
with unerring aim
towards the inhospitable;
no faith withstands it.
My daughter slept
folded into sharp corners;
she dreamt that hope fragments.
The rising sun kindled the scales
of dragons still gathered outside.

Shawn Aveningo

Binders Full of Women

> "... and they brought us whole binders full of women."
> – Mitt Romney, U.S. Presidential Debate, October 16, 2012

It wasn't until after the attack
I discovered the binder. Forty-seven

girls drugged, stripped, photographed,
raped. Page 48 sits empty, waiting

for the photo they took of me. Greek
Council enforced crackdown on hazing,

but for this, Sigma Chi had no such
policy. Buried beneath public

philanthropy and brotherhood, lie
bones of broken sisters, shattered souls,

shards of shame—a mosaic whose mortar
weakened year by year, one woman bravely

blowing the lid off the coffin.

Darlene Pagán

The Figurehead

Despite the row of maples like arrows sunk
beside the street, the locust on our lawn
reaches up and through them like

an imprisoned elderly neighbor waving
to passersby who never wave back. Though
it's early spring, her limbs sag in the full sun,

the nubs of bark swollen joints, the new
buds a dusty yellow as they curl into themselves
like fingers on arthritic hands. One neighbor

has suggested a different home for our tree
like the wetlands beyond the property where
the sunlight enters in threads and spots

and coyotes hunt for dim-witted cats and small,
wheezing dogs. Another suggests the recycle bin.
And though I'm not sure even I want her

rooted in the front yard like an out-of-season
ornament, I have adopted her as a reluctant
daughter-in-law might, have listened to complaints

against her, offered condolences as she stares
like a figurehead launched from a ship
baring her breasts, daring me to do otherwise.

Lois Rosen

Aurelia Aurita: Moon Jelly

No one cares about undress in the sea
Milky pink lingerie can't camouflage
my stomachs and radial canals
Aren't we all
water-filled
animals

Diaphanous parachute transparent moon
I contract
and expand
contract
and expand
no heart
spine
eye
ear
nor anxious brain

Muscle pulsation flings
plankton shrimp mollusks
against
my mucal skin

I sway delicate flagellate solicitation
but
don't think
you can grab
or
fondle me

Call me Medusa Saucer Umbrella
Silk Camisole
Belle

I lurk below your ocean's shallow rim
No spearless Lolita
venomous
I sting

Jodie Buller

Starfish Time

Up close in the summer
riding the backs of the sandstone boulders
as the waters rise slow in the cove,
the starfish seem sewn like patches
overlapping the barnacles
leaking salt in the long wait
from tide to tide.

We placed our last things
on a hump of stone
and wandered out thigh deep
in the Sound. At our feet
the water clear, a colony
of orange and purple, fresh submerged
stirring to life.

So many fingers
I wanted to lay my body down
above them, float on my back
in the sun-warm shallows
taking in the shoreline upside down
the sky a blue bowl
rimmed in gold and green.

I wanted the ocean moving beneath me
rocking my limbs in a salty lullaby.
I asked if you were ready
and you wanted to be so you said yes,
but it wasn't true yet, what you wanted;
You were still straddling the shore.

In an underwater movie with sped-up time

the starfish move in teeming hordes
they cover ground like colonies of ants on land.
Our short immersion into their time zone
was only a sea breath, a cilial possibility
the beginnings of grace.

There's a man in Costabel
on a coast that calls shipwrecks
who steps out into the early low tide
and plucks stranded starfish from the rocks
where they cling, pitching them
through the waves into the hurling sea.
Have you been him?
Have you, too, longed to enter the intertidal zones
with your heart pumping
and your limbs working
on some inexplicable urge
to save whatever life moves you?

You can watch it all, see it very clearly,
but without that spark of irrational love
—the one that asks you to shift speeds
and feel from beyond your particular time—
without that urge to submerge yourself
in the world, don't hope to know it yet.

The world unfolds only as the heart learns
too, and the heart—the heart is a starfish
it covers ground without seeming
to move, sometimes.

Four

Jennifer Kemnitz

Under the sign of the water bearer

And so the poles melted, engulfing all.
Water enfolded the low places, caressing
At first, cajoling, then push, shove, displace,
Like a large aunt when you don't take her hint,
Then she hip-bumps you over on the couch.
She gets what is hers, at last, as is right.

All in the way was inundated, absorbed
Into the great body of the ocean:
Her swells, her squalls and her gentle, sparkling calms.
Those living waters fed on the dead.
There were delicate things seen no more
And sturdy ones that cracked, split wide open.

All that she found she welcomed, she accepted;
All yielded under her steady persuasion.
The anger, guilt, sadness she washed over;
She had only joy to move and to spread,
Anointing the world's tired, dusty feet,
Diluting poisons, baptizing anew.

Cindy Stewart-Rinier

Polaroid of My Mother

There you are in your coral-colored pantsuit,
1972, though your spray-stiffened hair holds
something of the '60s Sophia Loren glamour
as you knead the bread dough from which
your eyes have momentarily risen.

Your mouth is a candid startle, slightly open,
perhaps on its way to *Don't!* or *No!*
Your deflection a reflex. You leveraged
weight into the heels of your palms, pushed
the pale belly of dough into itself and away.

The rhythm of roll, fold, turn, roll, fold, turn,
movement and reposition a pattern, a practice.
I've never forgotten the thing you told me
later that day, long after the camera came down
to hang slack by its strap at my side. I wanted

to know if you were all right in the aftermath of your
latest fight with my stepdad. You lifted the tea towel
from the top of the bowl, punched down the doubled
dough, the air escaping like a thousand exhalations.
The madder you are, you said, *the better the bread.*

Margaret Chula

Still Life with Cabbage

In the yellow kitchen, the cabbage is boiling. The pot is black where flames have bruised it. A woman is wearing a bib apron, her hair pulled back with bobby pins. The rubber ends are missing. They scrape her scalp when she sticks them in. Once she used to pin curl her hair before going dancing at the Bernardston Inn. Once she used to sing *It Had To Be You*. And then it was him. And then, five children wailing and burping and spitting up on her apron —the canvas one with the tie-on straps that harness her to the kitchen. She reaches for the ladle, thinking about the sheets, wet and clumped up in the washing machine. And then later, when her husband comes home, his silhouette dark and sullen beneath the covers, the whiskey breath that will make her gag and turn away. Now she's turning the hamburgers. The sizzle and spit sting her wrists. She wipes the grease on her apron, adding to the pigments of beets, pureed peas, and the swollen buds of Brussels sprouts that no one would ever touch.

Pattie Palmer-Baker

The Hand-Off

The speedometer trembles at one-twenty
but the Cadillac runs smooth, silent
as my father steers left-handed,
his right arm draped
over the top of the front seat.

I want to touch that blond-furred arm,
hold his fingers in my hand's hollow.

My mother leans to the right,
stares out the front window at the black asphalt
unwinding into the desert's lusterless gold.
She doesn't look at him or at me
or at the fifth of whiskey
amber-stilled next to her left foot.

Out the window to the left
a mountain presses purple up up
until lead clouds block the ascension
and through that metallic gray
God shoots silver shafts just for me.

Give me the bottle, Edith,
he says to my mother.
I see the dip of her left shoulder,
hear the slap of the bottle against his hand.
Her gaze never leaves the ochre-scrubbed sand.

He tilts the Jim Beam—
the scorched yellow liquid flows into his mouth.
I hear him gulp and swallow,
I see his fingers tender-curled around the bottle's neck.

In the mirror his crow's feet gentle and his dishwater eyes
flash a moment's burnished blue—
not for my mother not for me not for himself
not for the saffron sand or the purple mountain
but for the brown-gold whiskey.

Out the window—
still purple, the mountain—
and the white-gold slashing the stubborn gray,
not god-painted or angel-mounted—
a trick of the atmosphere,
a sleight of hand.

Victoria Wyttenberg

Three Rings at the Same Time and Performing Tigers

The flamethrower swallows the flame and I feel it
in my own throat and see it everywhere, burning orange and blue
on my hands, on stuffed animals given as prizes for hitting

the bull's eye. Flames lick the tent flap leading to the open
legs of the hermaphrodite then the mammoth tent.
Once, fire started on our rug when my mother opened

the woodstove door and released burning logs.
All our furniture marked by cigarette burns and circles
from sweating glasses. My son was only six

when he set a field on fire. My daughter wants things hot.
"If I'm going to eat," she says, "I want it fiery, want to feel
the burn, to taste Tabasco, red-hot pepper."

Mirrors go on weeping at bearded ladies, midgets,
the Rubber Man who changes shape with his moods.
Never too far from a small town, young girls

sell popcorn and oranges. A child is born into a landscape of copper
hills and a river but half a century later she could be anywhere
among the world's sounds. She might hear the laughing woman,

head back, send laughter straight up to the sky. Twenty-four
performing elephants, those overworked gods,
and rare wild beasts dream of jungle and river

as the ringmaster shouts, "On with the show!"
and the bareback rider floats above a white horse.
The tightrope dancer, always alone, can never look back.

The trick rider runs in circles. I smell sawdust and sweat
and join the Flying Wallendas, fearing only wind and burning canvas.
Eclipse, Forepaugh's thoroughbred, jumps through paper balloons

and rings of fire. Tumblers, eager to go a step further, take their act
to the backs of horses. They climb each other's bodies, form pyramids.
A lone woman ascends a ladder that remains vertical with no support,

a stunt she has been practicing all her life. The knife thrower
barely misses his partner's head with his shining blade and she thinks
of the argument they had this morning over a piece of fruit.

Like Mabel Stark, using neither whip nor pistol, I enter the lion's cage,
stroke his handsome head, his enormous mane and put my face
in his mouth. There are people who do not believe but keep watching,

keep taking wine and the tasteless wafer. We can all believe
in sorrow and want to be received at the table.
A trained pig plays "Home Sweet Home" on the xylophone

while a drunken sailor staggers for laughs and the sad clown
speaks French, his hair sticking out in all directions under his hobo hat.
Otto Griebling carries a block of ice, trying to deliver it

as it grows smaller and smaller and finally disappears.
Caramel corn, cotton candy, but life is not all spangles, bright
lights and tinsel. Roustabouts, that rough lot, stay strong

enough to survive a fall from the train and watch
red lights and their pay disappear up the tracks.
My mother dreams fire going everywhere like water,

glittery sparks flying, devouring our house like a tiger.
A handsome young man gets a buzz by juggling
three chain saws while I take plates from the cupboard

and spin them on my skull then lift an anvil with my hair.
My son breaks chains by expanding his chest.
My daughter learned the wire at ten and walks a tightrope

across Niagara Falls with baskets on her feet. If someone
gives us trouble we hurl him through a café window.
The lamp walks away and walls of the house have their own voice.

Meredith Stewart

Said & Meant II

after Li-Young Lee

When we said "interpretation"
you meant digging through the matter
of another's mind.

I meant bringing a gift to a queen.

You meant discovering a continent
after sailing through an ocean
of words.

I meant you can't find
what you don't already believe
is there.

You meant two plus two
and the rest is obvious.

I meant only four equals four.

You meant those who have ears,
let them hear.

I meant the ears
are what count.

You meant the sculpture
is already in the stone.

I meant hands in the clay
forming cups and we drink.

You meant the first dawn
breaking and witnessed
by peasants of the earth.

I meant Eve naming the animals.

I meant all that we create

the day after creation.

Wendy Willis

Violet at the Creation

In April, before the clouds settled
their differences and the lake was still
nervous, she crawled into the garden
while a blue-black bird resembling nothing

more than a catfish sang arias
to give her cover. The apple-hipped
stepmother taught her a secret
game to fool the husband

who wore an egg-yolk jacket
with *dominion* stitched on the chest.
The pie-apple bride tossed
her high and let her giggles

turned to pebbles dibblety drop
until the husband raised an umbrella.
They tried on names like rumpled gowns.
Nanny goat called herself sloth

and humpback whale was torn
between winter wheat
and passenger pigeon.
Falcon christened himself

something jeweled and unutterable,
while she blew spun glass
through the straw of her bones and plucked
her own name—Violet—from the new grass.

Annie Lighthart

The Hundred Names of Love

The children have gone to bed.
We are so tired we could fold ourselves neatly
behind our eyes and sleep mid-word, sleep standing
warm among the creatures in the barn, lean together
and sleep, forgetting each other completely in the velvet,
the forgiveness of that sleep.

Then the one small cry:
one strike of the match-head of sound:
one child's voice:
and the hundred names of love are lit
as we rise and walk down the hall.

One hundred nights we wake like this,
wake out of our nowhere
to kneel by small beds in darkness.
One hundred blossoms open in our hands,
a name for love written in each one.

Five

Dawn Thompson

Unexpected Conversation at Mid-Life

    fast flurry full
    go
    make it happen
    finish it up

    and there I am
    and there I'm not

    Kneel,
    says the Buddha,
    who I've never spoken to in my life.

    Bow,
    he
    says,
    and then continues on before I can interrupt him.

    When I sit cross-legged, he chants, *the world stops spinning,*
    slows
    stills
    sings.
    Do you see the way the sun tosses his light,
    a rose for your hair?
    he asks.
    Do you hear the opera of rain
    outside your window?

    Breathe
    Breathe
    Breathe
    he hums, looking pleased with himself
    I have to admit

he has my attention.

Ah, he laughs, satisfied.
That's all I've ever wanted.

Judy Beaudette

To Those Boarding Planes to Hawaii to Escape the Rain

You must not have seen what I saw this morning
after relentless rain of eight days straight:
A raven at the intersection of 81st and Alder

laid his cheek to the puddled pavement,
scooped rainwater into his beak

and tipping his head to the sky
he drank,
to a seagull, far above,
which screed and squinted in clouds
that opened their embrace to reveal
a small blue pond in the sky.

Oz Hopkins Koglin

On the Book

She's got to beg
"doc" the drug store man
to put the baby's medicine
on the book till payday
and she still owes
on the last time.

The old white man will
take the prescription all right
but she'll have to dodge
his quick hand touching
her young breasts—
handling change in the
colored part of town.

Bette Lynch Husted

How Can You Live There?

Driving home, I've hit that stretch of road
where the Gorge bares her shoulders, spreading wide
to possibility, but this time only coots
on the trapwater slough, no radio, plenty of time
to think of an answer were it not for sky—
lavender washing down to rose—and then for wondering
why it took me so long to discover coots. Line
of long-haul truckers looking, speaking sheep
on their CBs. How long did I drive by bighorns,
not seeing? Three turkey vultures, one remaining eagle.
Maybe he'll stay, welcome ospreys
and balsamroot. So many kinds of sage
I don't know. Yes, there are
far more important things.

When I leave the river, climb into hawk country,
horizons open. I could lie—shout out, "Ferruginous!"
or "Swainson's, juvenile!"—claim
an urban confidence, name something beautiful
besides these red-tails perched on every pole
common as dirt—though there are thirteen subspecies
I don't know—our histories
complex as breast feathers, kestrel
hover-hunting, highway plunging now toward town,
all scars and bruises and raw wounds
wrapped for evening in a shawl of Blues,
the foothills folding their loose-mottled weave
of canyon greens and shadows as if modesty
were virtue. Even truth. Or even close to home.

Kate Gray

Some Shelter

Outside the Lake Charles shelter for four thousand,
smokers gather, lean against wet walls, the heat
in the shade enough to raise sweat on knuckles.

In the stairwells, young men in Michael Jordan jerseys
cross bulging arms, their caps tipped to one ear.
To the one who stares me to standstill, I ask,
> *Is there anything I can get you?*

To this white girl in a red vest, he says,
> *Yeah, get me a house.*

The words come flat like bottle caps fired from fingers.

My Portland house, heaped with gardens, not gold,
looms beyond their reach. I could have walked,
Sorry, away. Instead to the question, I grab
my back pocket and say,
> *Just happens I have one right here.*

Their black eyes turn oval at my pantomime
of unfolding a deed. Then one man elbows another,
two slap palms, and smiles bounce
like pinballs on bumpers.
> *Baby*, they say, *that's rich.*

Pearl Waldorf

city spacious heart

in wind
in caged trees
in wet tire highway hush
perched at the edges
of front lawns repeating themselves

you are sparse dove
a keen reminder of the strange
being everything of infancy of being
an animal and not an animal at the same time

geese fighting for all the grass in the world

marching past milestones
these high glass boxes
these asphalt hills
train song
holding the place i am always going
i want my ocean back

gravity's simple blanket
skyscraping the only heaven i know
.

dreams of waves engulfing the city

Brandi Katherine Herrera

from *spoon*

[...]

chimney smoke
on the first days of summer
damp cedar plumes
pepper the air
like the first days of october
and i am wrapped
in a blanket on the porch
under the silver fir trees
with a silver-plated
dessert spoon
listening to the widower
next door
washing his dishes.

[...]

everywhere but here
people are tossing
feverish
in the sultry
while i'm listening
to the discernible clink
of silverware
against porcelain
rolling my spoon
around a dry mouth
remembering
homemade ice cream

its vanilla bean mystery

on the fourth of july
like alchemy
the magic of sugar
salt, ice, churned
until it was something
we could carve our spoons into
until it was dark enough
to light up the block
of ranches
and split-levels

with our sparklers
we spelled out names
like prism confetti
like handfuls of flung sugar
while our mothers
drank cane sugar cokes
with dark rum
out of the bottles
and sucked on marlboros
camels
winston lights
their tips glowing
like the dregs
of abandoned campfires.

one year
some drunk father
lit up our suburbs
with a wayward rocket
and we just stood there
with extinguished sparklers
quietly watching
the flaming arborvitae
lick the ten o'clock sky
our ice cream dripping
sugary punctuation

on the ash-peppered sidewalk.

in our burnt orange
corduroy cutoffs
we played
with pilfered matches
daring each other
to place palms
or fingers
over the flame's
open limnus
until the party died down
and our mothers
nervous
in high-waisted levi's
began to shift
in their lawn chairs.

the wind is picking up
as my neighbor coaxes a fire
and i'm still outside
in wool socks
thinking of the sorrow
of cherries flambé
baked alaska
pineapple
upside down cake
like sunspots
of some aged sweetness
i stir my well of sugar
and remember ice cream trucks

rocket pops
all of the typical signs
of summer
as my neighbor
slips a clean spoon

into his coffee
i measure the steps
to a dark bed
both of us
waiting out the night
like stray dogs
under the cool shadow
of parked cars.

This is an excerpt from *spoon*; the full version can be found online at:
http://voicecatcherjournal.org/2012FallIssue/poetry11.html

Favor Ellis

Trucker's Atlas

I should have taken notes, sketched landmarks. Left breadcrumb trails and taken cartography classes. There have been so many long roads. Shortcuts I took only when my palms would itch at the thought of detour. People could benefit from that sort of atlas, I think. The record of back roads we managed to take, one end to the next, with or without disaster. People need that kind of information.

People need to know which road always washes out by which stand of trees. Which day, week, month you can be sure to see which creatures behind which shadows. People ought to be able to make informed decisions.

I have some information.

I know that ten-mile stretch where you can turn your radio dial to the in-between station and be guaranteed to hear a song that will break your heart. I know about the woman who leaves hot biscuits on the bench by her mailbox. I don't know who she leaves them for. I assume they're for me, because they're always there, always hot.

I could tell you about the dirty old dog whose feet smell like toast, who loves to sleep in my cab from the town with the trees to the one with the water. She waits for me on the bank until I swing by to bring her back to the shade of sweeping branches.

There's the one stretch, the wide plain between the sun on the tallest tree, and the moon on the smallest hill, where I roll down my windows and holler out whatever old songs come into my head. That's how I first met the toast dog—she heard me singing and came running through the brush, hot biscuit in her mouth swiped from the bench down the way.

I taught myself how to sing on these roads. And I've memorized poems, long wordless tributes to the women I've loved. I especially like the poems I've written for the woman I've only seen once, fifty miles fast past, she never even knew I was here.

I should have been more forward thinking. Known how much it would be needed. Everyone needs a map. And if I'm the first one on these roads, or the first with a pen handy, I'm doing you all a disservice sitting in my truck, humming, eating biscuits, tracking the movements of the sky, when I should have been telling you what I know.

Six

Miriam Feder

Morning

> Awaken spirit
> Speak the smallest grains of truth
> Boulders will follow

Marj Hogan

Pump House

She went out in winter.

Winter, and she was already
done. She went out when the leaves
were almost gone.

All kinds of miles
to be alone. Grass spent and dry,
blackberry hard on the vine,

she stood by the pump house
and listened to the wind inside.
The whole of the valley

in a whistling room.
Wind at the boards. And the pump,
the black pond, each bent reed

drowning its half-moon
told her to tremble. How the pump
made its little sigh, hollow.

Hollow clouds and hollow sky.
Water will shallow and ice over,
but that will be later. For now it keeps

pumping. She hears the old wood,
this cold wind, and somewhere under,
a dull, soft thumping.

Penelope Scambly Schott

Anticipation

is the far apart birthdays of early childhood

is the shut buds of the scarlet rhododendron
before each bud peels itself open into a sunrise

is awaiting the moment when socks are sorted
and spoons are with spoons, forks with forks

is my methodical husband buzzing his toothbrush
a precise two minutes before tossing his skivvies

into the wicker hamper
is the sound of wicker shutting on wicker

is him looking at me as if I were a happy surprise
in his bed

is his soft snoring
and a warm pocket of air around flesh

and the low *ta-thump* of his heart
is some unknown night

when there is no *ta-thump*

Pat Phillips West

Decomposition

Days grow longer, she finds her husband
wandering around a neighbor's back yard
after dusk. *I'm on my way to Boise*, he says.
No mention this time about jumping out of a hatch
in the moon. She gets him home, tucks him in.
He grabs her hand, *Do you understand*
the importance of keeping death
on the left side of the bed?

Late summer, he leaves a forty dollar tip
for a lunch of half that amount. He reads
for thirty-six hours straight—Edison, Ford,
Lindberg, and Firestone—says, *Hymens*
and hymnals protect holy stuff
sweet to the ears and to the touch.

Days shorten, sun sits low in the sky. He declares,
I need to check my mushroom crop, crawls
under the bed. She locks the dead bolt,
hides the key. He finds it, opens the front
door, runs out naked in a rainstorm, curls up
under a hydrangea bush. She takes his arm,
tries to pull him up from the muck.
He bites her hand.

Heidi Schulman Greenwald

Caring for Father

She strokes stitches on his abdomen, a trail
traversing ribs that wraps around his back.
Outside, two men ply his yard, pointed shovels
digging trenches. They skirt lilies, yellow buds
still lingering. Lavender unearthed, roots to sky.
She inquires. *Leak in the sprinkler system,*
one man replies. He checks irrigation pipes, she thinks
knife through skin, gliding past intestine, skirting
riven lower rib, liver, to staunch bleeding. *I've got it.*
She looks up, sees the second man, a faint spray before
his face. The men heave clay to trenches, tamp
lavender back home. One branch buried under earth.

Burky Achilles

'A'ā

for my mother, July 1, 1936–April 6, 2013

It is time for winter swell
to pull back and crest
into one perfect
wave of understanding
between us, the way tide
understands the moon,
the way you knew
when to add more limu
to the poke,
when the first honohono
orchid would bloom.

It is time you told me
about your sister Marilyn,
her years in the institution.
About your red tricycle
circling and circling
the flat driveway
of your childhood home
after the deputy told your mother
that electroshock had cauterized
the wound of your sister's mind
and stilled her heart.

Time's puzzle is how to fit
your ocean
into my thimble.
Being not seen and not heard
let me skulk
like a thief around

corners, behind
walls, collecting
enough snippets to set
the razor-straight edges
of your thousand-piece life.

Winter swell honors no time,
gives no quarter to my dog paddle
through undertow,
between the jagged 'a'ā rocks,
to shore's sun-bleached sand
where you wait, warm towel in hand
for my shivering body.
It is time to puzzle why
you never swam out to meet
me. Why, when I was the one
being swept under, you,
feet firmly planted
on shore's warm sand,
were the one who needed
saving.

Jennifer Liberts

Bridge

Sometimes I stand at the kitchen window
watch my neighbor pulling weeds in his yard
and say how are you how are you.
Sometimes I stand at my kitchen window
and wave to couples walking their dogs
and wonder how they live with all that hair.
I say what kind of dog is your dog
did you hear the frogs going on all night
do you need me to take care of your mail
your trash your child your lover your hydrangea
as I scrub the kitchen off the plate
watch the red bits and dish soap
run down the drain. Sometimes
I wave and they wave and I turn away
and they keep walking down the street,
through the park, into the small Colonial
around the block. When you jumped
off the bridge I was putting away the salad
dressing, loading the dishwasher,
wiping the countertop with an old blue rag.
I wonder if you saw the reflection of the man
rushing toward you in that cold clear
rippling water. If you waved
at him and he waved right back.

Alice Hardesty

Tango Club—Valparaiso

The accordionist is too feeble to get up
between numbers. The singer,
square and solid of body, ends each song
with a vibrato wavering toward flat.

Only the old couple braves
the tiny dance floor. His thick hair gleams white,
hers a faux strawberry blonde, eyes faded,
jaw resolute above a thickened neck.
Her body shaped by empanadas and many children
is adorned by a white-sequined jacket,
black skirt with long side-slits,
and high-heeled tango shoes.

Together they glide like an ancient boat
in a smooth sea. Weathered hands
on ample backs, foreheads nearly touching,
they twist slowly, leg over leg,
torsos resisting the seduction
of undulating hips.

Head bent slightly forward, he smiles
throughout. Survivors, grateful
to be no longer young,
they have set aside all memories
of tanks and guns, his long absence,
the temptations of despair. The boy
who never came home lives
in the narrow space between them,
silent for now.
For now, only the dance.

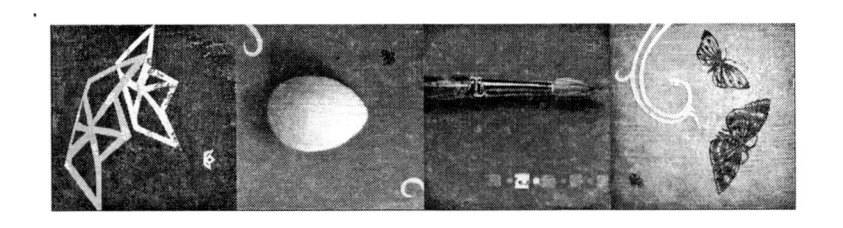

Seven

Sage Cohen

More Like Music

We all need a line against which
to measure our wildness.

The park is cut back along the path.
I align my spine with the heavy bench,

send my legs out around your waist
as the sun heats a halo through your long black hair.

Today I can understand how the scientists misjudged
the universe's color for turquoise when really it is beige.

The sun must have been streaming through the trees
such that the calculation of space divided by matter

became more like music. And when the rhythm lifted
like a woman's skirt in summer wind, someone sang,

as you do now, of the sky being cleared by a good hard rain.
Then the universe compressed like two bodies dancing,

perfected with the pressure of exchange, until
the planetary percussion became a salsa.

Leaning into the beat, those men reached further
than who they were. Surrendered fact to abstraction.

They got loose in their laboratories, pressed to the truth
of the blue of turquoise until it was the only answer.

Toni Partington

The Fujita Scale*

she is a storm chaser
who seeks the thrill
inside electrical strikes
and sheets of rain

her life defined
by movement toward the funnel cloud
fed by spirals of energy and dust
and someone's roof

he spills into her life
like rain through a cracked foundation
at 200 miles per hour
an F-2 on the Fujita Scale

his power bends her will
chasing his wind becomes her folly
as it roars above
and below her soul

their love a vortex
on an empty road
sanity spinning
farther away

his nature uncontrolled
    like a fault line
    a rockslide
    a firestorm

his fist
unpredicted

at 400 miles per hour
an F-4 on the Fujita Scale

by then
> doors slam
> glass flies
> pieces of insulation blow away

yesterday, she was a storm chaser
seeking the thrill
inside electrical strikes
and sheets of rain

today she watches the weather
behind curtains, sheer and muted blue
as he waits behind bars
for the day she will drive him home in the rain

---

*The Fujita Tornado Intensity Scale is used to measure the strength of a tornado based on the damage it produces. It typically consists of six ratings from F0 to F5, with damage rated as light to incredible.

Amy Schutzer

To the Friend Who Talked Me Down

She did not say
do this, do that
or whether I was listing
right or wrong.

The knowable heart
is an hourglass;
love, an elevator going up
going down,
that was the gist
of what she said
on the sidewalk
with the April sky divided
between sun and clouds bearing rain.

Jennifer Foreman

Relic

Your paint-stained hoodie still hangs in our closet
your ashes rest on the shrine of your nightstand
locals come by asking to hold your asthma inhalers
cats sleep on your pillow next to my head
bread crusts from your last sandwich are under a glass dome
beer you were drinking when you died is in the fridge
some spilled on the bottom shelf and I refuse to clean it up ever
I won't wash your dirty socks
I pray to your old hair ties
twisting the knotted hair strands with my thumb and index finger
chanting your nicknames
speaking in tongues when I think of the life we had
sweet saint of the working class carpenter big lug gentle giant
I pour whiskey on the ground and whisper your full name 27 times
Thomas Michael Palmer Thomas Michael Palmer Thomas Michael Palmer
I pace the floor waiting for you to come back
dress like you for Halloween
throw my hands up begging you to be my savior
deliver me from the absence of you
your nail clippings have been fashioned into a mobile
that hangs over my bed
I sleep in your underwear and large torn tee shirts
holding your truck keys
wake up to the sound of your voice
someday a stranger will find your sketch pad
and declare you a prophet
our apartment has become a stupa.

Emily Kendal Frey

Sleep

We make of sleep
packets of things.
The fragments
of what we've seen.
Instead of a carousel
of sound and horses
I think we divide
night into light-shaped
bows to be fitted
with arrows
of what we know.
Tuck them in with us,
keep them safe.
To be used
later, when awake.
Some people want
shores of planks and nails
instead of the white
curve of a sail.

Barbara LaMorticella

A Passing Music

For one moment
all of you gathered
into sharp gleaming darkness
a movement like a boat
      cutting the light
  from the light

Little mysterious sound
On a summer day
      of something
    (but it's gone already)
breaking the surface of the water,
the sign of it only a
passing
    music . . .

Forever after, I will remember
this sudden abstraction of you, this you
profound and simple as a needle,
sewing the margins of two
kingdoms.

Paulann Petersen

Solder

    Today's laminate card says
    this man is deaf, will I buy
    pencils, 3 for 2 dollars, 5 for 3.
    He waits at my door. *Sham* a possible
    sham, but this winter day is vernal-bright,
    two dollars little enough. *For shame*. No one,
    for years, has come to my door peddling
    so little. Decades ago, on a city bus,
    a sign thrust itself at my eight-year-old eyes:
    PLEASE BUY. The needles for sale
    stitched themselves in pyramid steps
    through a square of red foil,
    the magic threader standing at apex,
    silver queen, scepter-shaped.
    Those hands urging the needles
    might have, with a broken-winged flutter,
    made words, but were held
    wordless as I. The left hand offered
    those gleaming one-eyed needles,
    the right held the 3x5 card
    pleading with me to buy. That a deaf-mute
    wanted so long ago so little from me,
    a child with hearing, my voice close at hand;
    that my allowance, a weekly quarter,
    stayed in my fist, warm solder
    to my grip: a small but indelible
    shame. From today's hand I pick
    three silver pencils shiny as wands,
    that hard flesh on their ends
    the blue of this February's
    boundless day. Cheap,
    the erasers leave on a page
    streaks of sky darker than
    whatever mistakes they replace.

Melanie Green

Talking Herself into Onward

Let go
the with-holding
and treble shy.

Unbind the mind's
flounce.
Unflinch bungle and say.

Leave
the worry-huckster,

the universe thrums.

Stride on,
forward the hope-gamble,
muscle
with faith.

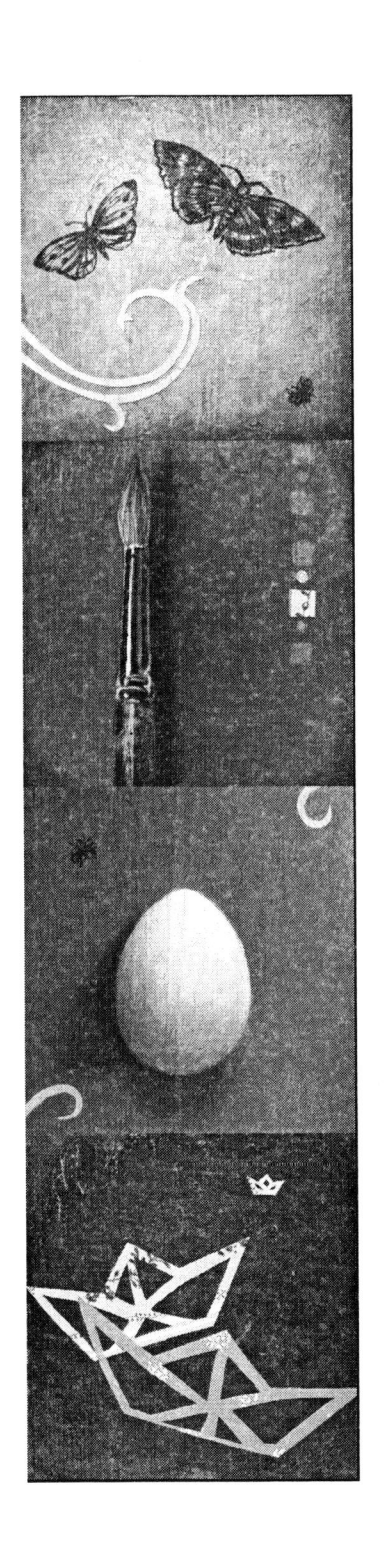

Prose

From the Prose Editor

Twenty-Two Stories about Us

An old Hasidic saying goes, "If I tell you my story, you will listen for a while and then you will fall asleep. But if, as I tell you my story, you begin to hear your own story, you will wake up."

Readers selected twenty-two prose pieces for this anthology from over 150 that have been published in *VoiceCatcher* since its inception in 2005. From one line of a piece from this anniversary anthology, you might recognize a story you know well:

There were other fires of childhood, stoked by a father who hit a mother.

I was the dance team leader, a setter on the volleyball team, a princess at the prom, and I was a slut.

I'd never been alone with a dead body.

I spent my life trying to get my father's attention and approval and now it's too late.

This is what we want for our children, that they grow up to be independent.

He said get your affairs in order, Joan, you have about four weeks left.

I couldn't get enough of Sarah, her smell like lavender and ylang ylang, her taste like popcorn and marshmallows.

Among these pages, you'll be prompted to rediscover buried grief, private treasures, familiar anxieties, and abiding passions. As you listen to each individual writer's voice, you might find what Trista Cornelius experiences as an urge to embrace the other and "to acknowledge, 'We're here! You and me, out in this! No one else.'"

Many forms are represented in this gathering of twenty-two including flash forms, historical fiction, reportage, and haibun, a form that includes a scene in prose or prose poetry and ends with a haiku. And, unless you know something I don't know, you won't definitively be able to distinguish the fiction from the nonfiction either. Before *VoiceCatcher*'s first online edition in fall 2012, each prose piece was marked "story" or left undifferentiated from poetry in the table of contents. I appreciate what Sara Guest wrote in her introduction to *VoiceCatcher* 3, "Women forgot to tell us what kind of story, what genre. We realized, as we read and read: it doesn't matter."

Here, in this collection of *VoiceCatcher*'s most compelling prose from the past ten years, there are, indeed, stories that we can embrace without specifically categorizing them, women's voices that have the power to wake us all up as we hear—and recognize—these are our stories.

Judith Pulman
Prose Editor

One

Jill Elliott

Robins

It was early spring when I phoned Aunt Glen and Uncle Peter to tell them I had to change my flights from Portland to London. I doubt Glen remembered I'd planned to visit them. By this time, little migrated from her short- to long-term memory, so I was surprised when she commented about the airports being closed.

"It's all that volcanic ash, isn't it?" she said, "It's on the news."

"That's right. The planes can't fly through it. It's not just England either. It's over most of Europe."

"It's on the news. Volcanic ash. When are you coming to see us?"

"Next month I hope. I have to reschedule my trip."

"Are you going to stay with us?"

"I'd like to, for a few days."

"You know where we live now, don't you?"

"Trowbridge." I knew she'd forgotten the name of the town. She usually called out to Peter to ask where they lived. "You used to live in Peacehaven, by the sea."

"Yes," she sighed as if she missed those days, "by the sea." She chanted an old rhyme: "A sailor went to sea, you see / To see what he could see, you see / And all that he could see, you see / Was sea, sea, sea."

Had she done it again? Had she somehow read my mind and transformed my unspoken thoughts into words, or was it merely the word *sea* that triggered the ditty? I had not told anyone in my family in England that my son, Trevor, was seriously considering joining the United States Navy. I suppose it could have been a coincidence, but my aunt had made other comments about missing the sea, and this was the first time this particular rhyme had popped out of her mouth. It reminded me of the time she pulled the word *lazy* from somewhere to describe the core of my ex-husband.

As Glen repeated her sailor ditty for the second time, I noticed a commotion in my back garden. The robins were attacking a squirrel that had climbed too close to their nest. With wings flapping, they warded off the predator. Parents try to protect their young, but what can you do when they reach adulthood and make their own decisions?

After I'd lost count of the number of times Glen repeated her sailor ditty, she said, "What? What do you want?" with a rare sharpness in her voice.

"Well, I wanted to tell you that I've had to postpone my trip to see you."

"Not you, Peter. He's pointing his finger at me and I don't know what he wants."

"Maybe dinner's ready and it's time to eat."

"You're probably right," she said, calmly. "He does like to feed me. Peter does all the cooking now, you know. I just sit and wait."

"I think you should keep this husband, Aunt Glen."

"I think I will," she said. I could hear the smile in her voice.

After we'd said our goodbyes and hung up our phones, I wondered if Aunt Glen would remember who had called.

❖ ❖ ❖

A few days before the phone call, Trevor and I had been sitting outside the Bagdad Theatre sipping our dark beers when he told me he was thinking of joining the military.

"You're joking, right?" I stared into his hazel eyes. He shook his head but didn't move his gaze from mine.

"What about going back to college? What about doing something with your massage therapy license from Michigan? Don't you remember Robert from the Unitarian Church? He said you had healing hands." I noticed my own hand shake as I reached for my drink.

"Mom, I've got friends with huge college debts. I'm not going to do that."

"So, this is all about money?"

"Lack of money. I'm sharing a house with three other people. I have no extra cash and I don't want to live the rest of my life like this. I don't want to end up like Dad."

Trevor had lived one long Michigan winter with his father, my ex-husband, in a house with no gas or electricity. They'd cooked meals on a camping stove. Trevor, who was attending college and had a part-time job, had paid for his father's medications and their food. He didn't earn enough money to pay the mortgage or heating bills and his father was unemployed. After the pipes froze and thawed, the basement flooded. In early summer the house was repossessed.

Trevor only told me the details of that winter after he'd moved to Portland. He found a job at Walgreens, and was promised more pay and a manager's position after a year. That didn't happen. Instead the recession worsened.

"What about the Peace Corps? You're a gentle soul," I said, remembering the peace marches I'd attended, and the Unitarian church we'd both been involved in.

"They only take people with bachelor's degrees. I've only got my associate's," he said, stroking his scruffy beard.

"Coast Guard?"

"Checked that out. They want people straight out of high school. I don't want to be in the Army or the Marines. I've talked to recruiters at the Navy and the Air Force."

"You've already talked to recruiters?" I stared into my beer, unable to lift my head in case the moisture in my eyes pooled into tears. This was serious. He'd probably considered all his options. I realized then he'd already made up his mind, and talking to me about his decision was the last of his hurdles. This is what we want for our children, that they grow up to be independent. But we also want them to be happy, and no matter how he argued, I couldn't believe my gentle son could be happy in the military.

"Your father was in the Navy and your stepfather was in the Air Force, so I guess you'll please one of them." I couldn't keep the bitterness from my tone. Was this my fault?

"If I get into the Navy I want to be a medic. One of their ships went down to Haiti, to help out. And yeah, Mom, I remember what Robert said."

As well as his healing hands, I reminded myself that Trevor had never possessed the fear gene. He was born with the umbilical cord wrapped loosely around his neck, and I sometimes wonder if he is fearless because he survived that first ordeal. Before his fifth birthday, he climbed onto the back of the couch, placed the curtain pull around his neck, and jumped to the floor. At the lake, he flipped himself upside-down while wearing a swim-ring. I only noticed he was in trouble when I saw his legs waving in the air. He taught himself to swim by toddling out into the lake until the water reached his neck, lifting up his chubby legs, and kicking. Once he put his sister's broken bracelet into an electrical outlet and burned his hand badly. I had breathed a sigh of relief when Trevor safely reached the age of twenty-five.

❖   ❖   ❖

Aunt Glen and I had followed similar paths. We'd both married young, divorced, remarried, and had two children. I sometimes worried that my life would mirror hers. Her son, my cousin Steven, died when he was twenty-four. He hadn't been in the military. He'd fallen from the window of his third floor flat. For years at the anniversary of Steven's death, Aunt Glen actually lost her voice, as if it were too painful for her to talk about her son.

"Earth to Mom," Trevor waved his hand in front of my face, getting my attention the way he'd done for years.

"Have you signed any papers yet?"

"No, I wanted to talk to you first."

"You've told your father?"

He nodded.

"And he's probably thrilled, right?"

He nodded.

"So, if you sign up, how soon do you have to leave?"

"It takes a while, two or three months I think. There are tests and tons of paperwork, and they might not even take me."

There was my thread of hope; maybe my son wasn't good enough for them.

I felt as if I'd failed a motherhood test by not being able to talk him out of signing up. I remember Mum telling me that Glen would sit and talk with Steven about his latest brush with trouble. He'd listen to her advice, appear to understand, and then do whatever he felt like. That's like many of the discussions I'd had with Trevor over the years. Do the women in our family have voices that are listened to but never truly heard?

A few days later, I walked outside to my garden, my refuge and my place to ponder and write. The turquoise eggs in the robins' nest had hatched. I sat quietly on my patio chair, while the father robin returned to feed the babies. High-pitched squeaks filled the air as beaks opened and reached upward for food. Once the father left, the babies settled down again and were quiet. The adult robin flew to a high branch on a neighbor's tree. From his perch he looked down on a crow, drinking from the birdbath, until the crow had quenched its thirst and flown away. It was only then that the robin flew back to earth to forage for more worms to help feed his family.

Within a few weeks I'd rescheduled my trip to England and my son had signed the next five years of his life over to the U.S. Navy. I had tentatively begun telling a select few people but I really didn't want to talk about my son. The wound was too raw. I suspected people would offer sympathy, which I didn't want, or advice, which I wouldn't heed. It would be worse than when I was pregnant, when strangers told me horror stories of forty-eight-hour labors while smiling and placing their hands on my distended belly. I dreaded the stories of sons who had joined the military, stories of sons who returned horribly maimed and unable to take care of themselves, or sons who were carried aloft in flag-covered coffins.

I found myself preparing Trevor's favorite foods in case he stopped by. I kept ingredients for hummus on hand so I could make a quick batch to snack on while we talked. I bundled leftovers for him to take home, trying to nourish him while I still could.

The Sunday before Trevor was due to leave for boot camp, our small family sat on the patio and gorged on fajitas, one of his favorite summer meals. He and I had cut, marinated, and grilled peppers, onions, zucchini and mushrooms, while my daughter chopped tomatoes, avocados, and onions to make guacamole. We drank beer and wine while we prepared the food, and munched on black corn chips and spicy salsa.

We took pictures of each other and the robins, which were almost too big for their nest. They filled their soft space and one, probably the largest, would sometimes stretch its wings and flap. Adult birds stayed away while we noisy humans ate and drank. When we went inside for dessert of strawberries, ice cream, and seven-layer cookies, the birds returned to feed their young.

The next morning, I settled into the patio chair, writing unspoken fears in my journal. Over the years this process had helped, but worry will empty a lot of pens and fill many books. The sound of wings flapping broke my brooding. I glanced up to see a young robin fly for the first time. It flew about ten feet and landed on the trellis where wisteria and winter jasmine climb. The second bird fluttered from the nest to a branch of the hydrangea less than a foot away. With frantic flapping of wings, the robins called to each other with deeper chirps than before. Was one calling the other back to safety, or was it daring its sibling to fly farther? Eventually the braver bird flew to the midst of a Douglas fir and hid amongst needles and cones.

The mother robin returned to the nest, a worm dangling from her beak, and found it empty. She cocked her head towards the sound of chirping, hopped up a few branches, and then bent her head to feed her last baby. Then she flew to the far corner of the back garden. The fledgling followed and landed, safely, on a cedar branch. I watched as the mother flew between the ground and cedar over and over again. She never landed on the branch. She was trying to encourage her youngster to follow her to the ground, so she could teach it how to peck for insects and worms and how to take care of itself.

❖   ❖   ❖

Eight months have passed. It's time to plan my annual trip back to England, to phone Aunt Glen and hope that she still remembers me. Recently, she's forgotten Steven.

Trevor survived basic training in Illinois, attended classes in medical care, and spent time in Michigan with his father and friends. He visited Seattle and Portland for two weeks in December. He and I strung holiday lights under the patio cover, drank beer again outside the Bagdad Theatre, and baked seven-layer cookies. While snacking on hummus, we made his favorite cold-weather meals: aloo saag, vegetable biryani, shepherd's pie, cauliflower cheese, and wild mushroom soup. Now he's at Camp Pendleton in California being trained by the military. This morning, as I unwound the outside lights, I smiled when I noticed fresh yellow grass swirled around the inside of the robins' nest. I have to believe that if the robins return, so will my son.

Jennifer Springsteen

Stoop

Tanya and her man lived in the upstairs apartment of the townhouse and I had the ground floor. We both had back porches that looked onto the alley, but we shared the front stoop. The front stoop was the place to sit and drink beers and watch people and cars pass.

Tanya was the first person I had known up close and neighborly who was taking female hormones and considering a full-on sex change. She had played basketball in high school, and the muscle tone in her shoulders and biceps had the permanent chisel of the eighteen-year-old boy she now wanted to hide. I could see the buds of two small breasts under her tight leotards, but the coarse black hair clung steady to her forearms.

Tanya's man never sat on the stoop. He hardly ever said "hello." Even to her. He just scowled a lot. I figured it was because he was a regular guy with boots and a metal lunchbox and a construction job, and I knew his secret. "That's just his way," Tanya explained like someone's grandmother. But they always had big fights. I could hear them screaming and throwing things and then there was crying. Sometimes the crying sounded like screwing. Maybe it was both.

The biggest fight ended with the man stomping down the stairs and slamming the door so hard it sprung mine open. I snuck upstairs to check on Tanya. I'd never been in their apartment, but I figured on the layout being an exact match to mine. She was in the front bedroom sitting at a vanity between two wigs on Styrofoam busts. There was the brown relaxed cropped cut I'd always seen her in, and a long curly black one. Her own short nappy head sat in between her hands like a thing broken, needing support.

"Tanya," I whispered.

She put her head up and looked at me through the mirror. "Lord, girl," she said. She had a big shiner alright, and the eye inside all that blue puff was red-veined. Her lower lip was split, and I saw the washcloth on the dresser with the blood.

"You mean he beats you?" I asked incredulous. "Women try to get away from men like that and here you are . . ." I didn't know what it was I couldn't say. Big? Buff? A man? We looked at each other in the mirror. "Why?" I finally asked.

"He beats me 'cuz I ain't a woman."

"That's crazy. Fuck him! Why doesn't he just go find a damn woman then?"

Her tears were thick and clotted with mascara. "'Cuz he gay." And then quieter, "And 'cuz he love me."

I sat on my heels next her, picked up the washcloth, and blotted her lip. "Next time, you hit him back."

One time as we sat on the stoop, with a beer can in her right hand, Tanya ran the other across the front of my neck, into the concave space between my collar bones and laid it flat on my chest right above my breasts. Then she cupped the knob of my shoulder in her palm and kept her hand there as she turned and took a drink. I could see her Adam's apple ride up and down in her throat. How effortless it was for me to be a woman. It felt awkward to take for granted what Tanya wanted so badly. When I sensed she was about to pull away, I scrunched up my shoulder and pinned her hand with my cheek.

When old Ms. Patterson from down the block died, the niece and nephew took what they wanted, sold the house to the state and put a sign on the gate that said: *free inside*. Tanya and I went in to see what was there. I took some old children's primers and a blue oil lamp. Tanya got a cut-glass candy dish and some embroidered hankies.

"I don't want to go like that," she said as we walked back home with our loot, "all alone and worthless. White kids and faggots rooting through my personal shit." She started to cry. We sat on the stoop again. Weepy, she fingered her hankies, and I flipped through the primers.

"Good Lord, Tanya," I said when she didn't let up. I nudged her with my elbow. "How much estrogen have you been taking? You whine and complain like a damn bitch."

She smiled over at me. "Really?" she asked. The mascara trailed along her cheeks and down her nose. "Good. Shit's finally working after all."

Patricia Kullberg

Forget about Florence Nightingale
August 1941, Portland, Oregon

Maybe the hot spell was to blame. For days, the thick, stupefying heat had clamped down over the city. Phoebe wasn't used to it. The heat distracted her, made her lose track of herself and right from the start, her morning ran askew. She'd stationed herself in front of the isolation ward next to a small metal stand piled with pale green cotton gowns, burnt orange rubber gloves and white gauze masks, expecting a minute to collect and arrange herself, but down the corridor a herd of white-coated men rounded the corner toward her. In one quick motion she slipped her hand behind the stiff, concealing folds of her skirt, grasped a garter through the cloth and tugged it out of the dent it had dug into her flesh. Here she'd barely cracked her day open and her girdle already pinched and her heavy rayon hose felt as hot and prickly as the devil's payback.

The starched and puffed platoon pulled to a stop in front of her, the younger doctors jockeying for position around Dr. Sternberg. Dr. Ladd captured and held the Chairman's right flank. A tall, stooped man, Dr. Sternberg had red razor scrapes across his pale cheeks, a thin ring of white hair around the shiny dome of his head and tobacco-stained teeth. His eyes were blue marbles. He peered first at Phoebe's good eye, then at the one that turned in. For a moment he looked confused, as people often were, about which eye she used—both of them, of course, and as a medical man surely he should have known that. "Miss . . . ," he dropped his gaze and thrust his head forward to squint at the nametag pinned above the left breast pocket of her uniform, the way he did every morning, "MacIntire. Shall we begin?"

Phoebe grabbed a gown, mask and gloves for each doctor, covered herself, then heaved the door open onto the ward. Dr. Sternberg's nostrils flared as he stepped forward into the hot, stuffy room, weighted with the rank odor of sick children. Four small, twisted bodies, naked but for diapers, lay under a harsh white light on steel-framed cots and cribs. Their mewling cries fell on Phoebe's ears. The acrid smell of vomit stung her eyes. Beneath her long-sleeved gown, wet circles grew under her arms.

Esther straightened up from the corner crib and stood at attention. When Phoebe looked over, she flicked her eyes to the ceiling.

It was a safe bet Esther's appeal to the heavens was lost on the doctors, because they had already crowded around the first cot where Luke, a flushed and panting boy of four, lay grunting with each outward breath, his fine blond hair plastered to his scalp with sweat. The boy's back arched so far off the bed Phoebe could have slid her hand under the small of his back. His right lower leg was unnaturally drawn up and out to the side, the cords of his hamstrings standing out like three taut wires behind his knee. All his work to breathe produced precious little rise in his chest. He looked much worse than the afternoon before. Phoebe's poached egg on toast turned cold and leaden in her stomach. Another thing she wasn't used to was watching children die.

She wedged herself in at the head of Luke's bed to blot his brow with a cool, wet cloth, grateful that Dr. Sternberg did not order her out of the way, as he sometimes did.

"This boy," a fledgling doctor said, directing his remarks to Dr. Sternberg, "was brought to the hospital yesterday afternoon after thirty-six hours of fever followed by paralysis of the right leg." Beads of sweat popped out at the man's temples. "He's our fourth case of poliomyelitis meningitis this summer. He displays the classic arch in his spine of severe meningeal irritation. The quadriceps," he drew his index finger down over the front of the boy's thigh without touching him, "are paralyzed, allowing the unaffected and opposing hamstrings to pull the knee into rigid flexion. The—"

"Doctor," the Chairman said, "are you sure you don't have it backwards? Perhaps it is the hamstrings which are diseased and in *spasm*, pulling the leg into flexion against the healthy quadriceps."

The young man paled. "Spasm?"

Dr. Ladd elbowed him and stage-whispered, "Sister Kenny, the spasm lady."

Dr. Sternberg smiled and on cue, all the men laughed.

"Very good, Dr. Ladd," Dr. Sternberg said. "You will all recall the unorthodox theories of that nurse, Sister Kenny, from Australia." Dr. Sternberg lifted an eyebrow and looked at each of his underlings in turn. "Spasm, indeed. No such thing, never been proven. Now watch." With one hand he grasped Luke's knee and with the other tried to straighten the leg.

The boy let out a weak cry. Phoebe flinched and reached for his hot, grasping hand.

"There you have it, gentlemen," Dr. Sternberg said, "a most convincing demonstration of the resistance of the healthy muscle, the hamstring, to stretch."

He must have been joking. The knot in the hamstring was plain as day and the pain it caused the child was obvious. Phoebe scanned the fresh and earnest faces of the men above their masks, all pointed at Dr. Sternberg. Abruptly, Dr. Ladd shifted his gaze to her and, she later swore to Esther, twitched one eye at her, as if they shared a little secret. Flustered, she looked away.

Dr. Sternberg lifted his hands from the boy. "Sister Kenny would have us hot-pack these muscles. She claims it relieves the pain. Dr. Ladd, what might be the effect of hot-packing the body of a child with fever?"

"Exacerbate the fever, perhaps cause a convulsion."

Dr. Sternberg nodded. "Always be wary, gentlemen, of unorthodox theories."

The men made little snorts of assent.

Phoebe smoothed the bedclothes under the boy. He rolled his wide, glassy eyes to her without moving his head, as if his neck had hardened to stone. "Mommy," he whimpered.

Phoebe leaned into him, her throat full and throbbing. "Your mommy will be here soon, sweetheart, I promise." She'd tried to explain to Luke's weeping mother that parents weren't allowed onto the isolation ward, for fear of contagion. But, his mother pleaded, she'd already spent a day and two nights holding her child, what difference could it make now?

The truth was no one really knew how the poliovirus was passed. The doctors thought it leaked out in the spit or snot of the sick, propelled itself invisibly through the air and burrowed in through the nose of the unfortunate soul who wandered too close. But how they squared that idea with the fact that sometimes a nurse (though hardly ever a doctor), despite using a mask, still caught the dread disease. Phoebe had read about such cases back east in Chicago and New York and the stories laid a cold hand on the back of her neck as she worked with the children. The doctors weren't really sure how it passed from person to person. They guessed. Then they made up rules to fit their guesses and no wonder so many families refused to bring their suffering children to the hospital.

After they finished in the isolation ward, Phoebe shoved the gowns into a hamper in the hallway, punching them down with her fist and for a moment she lost herself in the satisfying way they yielded to her pummeling. By the time she looked up the doctors had nearly reached the door of the convalescent ward and Dr. Ladd, alone, was watching her over his shoulder with a puzzled look on his face. He had already turned away when she felt the heat rise into her cheeks. She hurried to catch up with them, waiting for her at the door. She tugged the heavy slab of wood open, avoiding Dr. Ladd's gaze. Inside the long, narrow room lay a dozen more kids with infantile paralysis.

It was the city's first brush with The Crippler in over a decade, more than twenty cases so far. Portlanders had awaited the disease the way a rabbit waits for the wolf—the beast was always lurking about. But until now they'd been spared the recurring summer horror of stricken, paralyzed children, not that they hadn't had enough to contend with—businesses floundering, not near enough jobs to go around, families flung out of their homes, a whole army of depressed and idle men wandering the streets. A dreadful time it had been. Just this past year the mood of the city had picked up after old Henry Kaiser and his son Edgar came to town to build ships in their harbor to feed the conflict in Europe. The war had done more to pull them out of their doldrums than any of President Roosevelt's policies about this or that, and Phoebe wasn't sure how to feel about that, to be thriving off someone else's misery.

The year she turned eight, 1927, was stamped in Phoebe's mind as the last year infantile paralysis came to prey on the children. All through that long, scary summer parents had hovered over their offspring. On the beach at Kelley Point Park, the families had gathered in small knots, the kids forbidden to mingle with each other. Grownups eyed her from a safe distance. *You look flushed, child,* they'd say or *you're limping,* in such accusatory tones Phoebe ran to her mother and asked if something was wrong with her. In hushed voices she was not meant to hear, her mama and papa argued over her. The sick kids were all from the rich side of town, her papa pointed out, and their girl was healthy and robust and damned if he was going to make her stay inside all summer. His view won out and neither Phoebe nor any of her friends got sick.

After '27, Portlanders sucked in their breath each June and held it until the first of August, when they figured they were home free. They might have had a few cases, but nothing alarming. Thrilled to have escaped once again, they sighed over articles in the *Oregon Journal* and its rival, the *Oregonian,* about cities and towns back east which logged hundreds of cases in a single summer, oh, the heartbreak of it. Not a few mused about how Portland must be doing *something* right, maybe keeping the coloreds and other riffraff out of town made the difference. Phoebe thought such ideas a whole bucket-load of nonsense and wore herself out thinking about why infantile paralysis had slunk back into their lives this summer. Things like this didn't happen for no reason at all. Her papa had set hard into her head that all things had an earthly explanation. Only sometimes, it wasn't so easy to figure out.

On the convalescent ward, an unnatural hush lay over the room smothering all but the tiniest sounds—the rustle of sheets, the squeak of rubber soles over the freshly waxed linoleum, the low murmuring of the nurses and the unceasing whine of the boy in the nearest bed. The children lay pithed onto the white sheets in exoskeletons of plaster, or steel and stiff leather, like a row of huge, dead insects. So many children and so quiet, it unsettled Phoebe. A high bank of windows over the beds looked west out onto a densely wooded hillside so close and steep not a single ray of sun ever penetrated into the room. Phoebe could tell they were in the thick of summer not by the quality of light, but from the stale, overbearing heat.

The whimpering six-year-old in the first bed was incased in plaster from his waist down, except for his diapered bottom. When the doctors approached he thrashed his head from side to side, pleading, "Take it off, please, it hurts, take it off."

Phoebe took his hand and he gripped her until his fingers blanched.

"Henry is now three days completely off the respirator and doing very well, as far as his breathing goes." The doctor raised his voice over the boy's cries. "Unfortunately both lower extremities are severely affected. Our plan is complete rest and immobilization for a period of three weeks at which time we will reassess the extent of recovery and splint accordingly."

The boy's eyes grew round, he filled his lungs and pushed out a high-pitched clatter of words. "Takeitofftakeitofftakeitoffl!" stabbing the air until Phoebe had to stuff a shriek back down her own throat.

The blank-faced doctors turned away in synchrony like a flock of birds and pushed through the stiff muslin curtains to the next bed. In it lay a thirteen-year-old bucktoothed girl with lank brown hair and close-set eyes. Dr. Sternberg took hold of the sheet she clutched to her chest. "Here we have an application of the new Toronto splint, designed to hold the lower extremities in a neutral position during the early convalescent stage."

The girl flushed. "Not now, doctor, please."

"There is nothing to be ashamed of, young lady." With a little flourish, Dr. Sternberg pulled the sheet from her grasp and stripped it all the way down to the foot of the bed. Her flaccid legs were strapped into an articulated steel splint, anchored around her waist with a thick, leather belt. The complicated contraption held her open in a frog-leg position. On a steel bedpan full of dark, stinking urine perched her bared bottom.

The men averted their eyes. Phoebe leaned across Dr. Sternberg to grab the sheet and whisk it up over the girl's nakedness. "Please excuse us, doctors. I'll clean the patient up for you."

They backed away and turned to the next bed while Phoebe pulled the pan from under the girl. The steel had indented the girl's buttocks with a ring of red. "Rhonda, you poor thing, you've been on the pan for a while, haven't you?" She looked away while the girl wiped herself, then helped her to replace the thin diaper-shaped cotton cloth between her legs and tie it together at her hips.

Rhonda clutched at Phoebe's arm, her lower lip trembling. "Do they have to come back today?"

"Maybe not, sweetie, we'll see." She pulled back the curtain, picked up the bedpan and turned, too abruptly, and bumped into Dr. Sternberg. Urine sloshed out of the pan and onto his oxfords.

She couldn't have done anything worse. "Oh! I'm so sorry! Wait, let me clean it up for you, please." She grabbed a towel from Rhonda's bedside and knelt to wipe the damp stain from the dark brown leather of his shoes.

Dr. Sternberg stood still for a few seconds before speaking. "That will do!"

Phoebe looked up as he pulled his eyes away from the opening at the top of her uniform and onto her face with a faint smile, as if he were still calculating whether the quick view of her fresh, pale bosom was adequate compensation for a ruined shoe, but was inclined to think it was. Dirty old man. Esther was right.

Henry, whose begging had never stopped, escalated his pleas into one staccato yelp after another. Forgetting about Rhonda, the doctors moved on. One of the nurses tried to quiet the boy, but Dr. Sternberg was forced to conduct the remainder of his rounds over Henry's screams and even his face twitched with each shriek by the time they finished forty-five minutes later, leaving a ward full of whimpering, agitated kids in their wake.

"Forget about Florence Nightingale," Esther had told her. A few weeks back, during coffee break on Phoebe's third day at the hospital, she'd led Phoebe to a corner table in the cafeteria. Esther Dunlap was sloe-eyed and had a way of talking that involved only one side of her mouth, as if the world were something she just had to put up with. "You know, all that crap about noble dedication and compassion and being an angel of mercy."

"But I want to help the children!"

"Sure you do, honey. We all do. But your first job on these wards is to play handmaid to the doctors and I have a hunch you aren't the type to take easy to that."

Phoebe wrinkled her nose.

Esther laughed. "A stink of a job all right and as the newcomer, you've got the worst of it. That's how Miss Hunnicut breaks her girls in, she makes them chaperone Dr. Sternberg and his minions on their morning rounds."

Miss Hunnicut was the head nurse, a diminutive woman who looked old as dirt and was just as hard beneath her fluttery, simpering ways. Phoebe couldn't tell whether Miss Hunnicut actually liked her or just wanted Phoebe to think she did.

"So let me give you a tip or two." Esther swept a chestnut-colored curl out of her eye and tucked it back under the wing of her white cap where the heavy pile of her hair was trapped. "Dr. Sternberg is fussy, squeamish you might say. I know, surprising for a doctor, but he's an orthopedic man and he strictly limits himself to bones and joints. He doesn't want anything to do with vomit or poop or pee. He likes his wards spotless and his nurses immaculate. Best way to deal with him, other than making sure all the spillage is cleaned up before rounds, is to give him a little peek down your top once in a while."

Phoebe lifted her chin. "I will not."

"Oh, don't be a prude. You got a nice set of knockers there and all Dr. Sternberg wants to do is look. Sex is too wet and sticky for him and at his age his pecker probably doesn't stand up anymore anyway, and I swear—"

"I'm not a prude and I don't care what Dr. Sternberg is capable of. I'm not letting him look at me that way."

Esther sat back and nodded. "Good for you then, you're not one to wiggle your tits or ass at a man to get something from him, are you? That's okay. You got yourself a guy?"

"Yeah, we're engaged."

Esther glanced at Phoebe's naked ring finger.

"Well, sort of." Phoebe had begged Mikky not to spend his precious, hard-earned dollars on a ring. What good would a ring do if they couldn't afford to live together? "We're saving our money and waiting to see what Roosevelt's going to do. I don't know what we'll do if we end up going to war."

Then like all Portlanders, they fretted over the war, how awful it must have been for those poor Londoners, imagine, any time of the day or night Jerry could swoop down and drop a bomb on you and nothing you could do about it except duck. What if the Japs gave them a taste of it right here, made sense they'd want to knock all those shipyards out. Good thing they had the Aircraft Warning System about set up, no dearth of volunteers, that was for sure, and did Phoebe know where to get some blackout paint on the cheap? Esther's folks needed it for the windows in their attic, no sense in buying heavy drapes for that dusty old space.

Phoebe shook her head. "I'm sick of war talk. So how about you, have you got a man?"

"I've got me a very sweet guy, three years old and he loves me like the dickens. His daddy wasn't so good at the loving part. He ran off and left us. Frankly? I'm glad to be rid of him." Esther found something on the other side of the room to focus on.

She didn't look so glad. Maybe Esther was that kind of woman who wanted to live closer to the truth than most men would stand for. But Phoebe liked the way she let fly with her words. "Lots of men around here," she said. "Maybe you could find yourself a rich doctor."

Esther turned back to her. "Nah, they're mostly taken." She gave a short laugh. "Except for Fletcher Ladd. Now there's one to watch out for."

"Is he part of *the* Ladd family?"

"That's the one. Dr. Ladd's not married yet so he's got a whole lot of romp in him. Any chance he gets he'll pinch your soft parts."

"Has he pinched you?"

"Nope. But I've heard stories. Just slap his hand if he gets too frisky. Best thing, though, is to steer clear."

But all the clear-steering Phoebe had managed hadn't worked to keep the man from winking at her this morning. Then he'd caught her pounding the linen. And spilling pee on Dr. Sternberg! As she rushed to the nurses' station after rounds she felt embarrassed all over again. It better not get back to Miss Hunnicut. Phoebe had more than one reason to keep on her sunny side. At the sink she thrust her rough and reddened hands into a hot stream of water. She worked up a thick lather and scrubbed herself up to her thin wrists with a brush of boar's bristle. Her hands always felt dirty since coming onto the polio wards. She couldn't seem to scrub them enough.

She found Miss Hunnicut at the counter poring over the work schedules for the following week. Two other nurses stood at the station, recording on charts.

"Luke Argyle, the little boy in isolation—"

Miss Hunnicut looked up. Her features were puckered together in the center of her face as if she'd just taken a suck off a lemon. She tended to blink a lot. Her iron-colored hair was pulled back into a French roll without a single wisp come loose under a white cap with wings so enormous Phoebe imagined a stiff gust of wind could carry her off. "Yes, quite ill, isn't he," Miss Hunnicut said.

"His mother is very distraught and I know I'm new here, but I don't see the necessity of barring parents from visiting their children in isolation."

Miss Hunnicut blinked and sighed as she laid her pencil down. She stood and motioned for Phoebe to follow. In a small waiting room, Miss Hunnicut closed the door behind them, sat on the sofa and tapped the space next to her. After Phoebe sat down, she reached over and patted Phoebe's knee. "So. What is the matter, dear?"

"I would like to let Mrs. Argyle see her child. He needs her."

"Now what does *isolation* mean?"

"To keep apart." Sunlight streamed in through the window behind Miss Hunnicut, making Phoebe squint when she looked at her shadowed face. "But is there really any reason I couldn't gown, mask and glove her so she could hold her boy? I'm afraid he's going to pass."

"Many new nurses make the mistake of becoming too emotional about the children."

"I'm not concerned about myself. I'm concerned about his mother."

"One of the duties of the nurse is to accustom parents to the hospital routines and shepherd them through a difficult time."

"I think," Phoebe said, "if she were allowed to see her boy, she would manage a little better."

"Mrs. Argyle must be psychologically insecure."

"Miss Hunnicut, her boy is dying."

Miss Hunnicut's blinking eyes rose to Phoebe's head. "Turn around, my dear, and let me adjust your cap."

Phoebe turned her head away and felt Miss Hunnicut's bony little fingers pick the pins from her cap, pull the loose, frizzy strands of her hair sharply back and re-fasten the hat, scraping the pins across her scalp.

"There you go." Miss Hunnicut stood and smiled. "Thank you for airing your concerns, Phoebe."

Phoebe followed Miss Hunnicut back to the nurses' station where she crushed half an aspirin into a spoon and mixed it with honey. This business with Luke's mom wasn't over yet. At Luke's bedside, all covered up again, she held the spoon between his parted lips, but his eyes had glazed over and he made no effort to take it. The honey dribbled over his lips and down onto his chin. She'd have to bring his fever down with a cool sponge bath, but wasn't sure how she'd manage it. The skin of fresh polio patients burned with the slightest touch. Maybe she could dribble the cool water onto him. She ran her eyes over his twisted body, gleaming with sweat. Another ruined child, one more stunned parent. These miserable wards, where the Great and Grand Doctors lorded it over everyone else.

"Poor little fellow." The voice behind her was low, muffled by a mask and much too close.

Phoebe spun around to Dr. Ladd, who stood so hard onto her she could feel the heat rise up off him. No other nurse was in the room. He'd trapped her between the bed, the bedside stand and his own solid self, his eyes fastened on Luke. He leaned over and with a small cloth he blotted away the tears trickling from the boy's eyes, the clear mucus oozing from his nose and the honey-smeared drool spilling out of his mouth. His fingers were long and slender beneath the tightly fit gloves and he performed these simple tasks with such delicacy and grace Phoebe sucked in her breath.

Dr. Ladd shook his head. "He won't take the aspirin, because he can't swallow and he needs every speck of concentration he has just to breathe, but you don't need me to tell you that, do you?" He reached out and took the spoon from her hand which Phoebe held out stupidly over the bed. "No point, really, in trying, is there?" He propped the spoon into a glass on the small stand. "So Miss MacIntire, Phoebe is it? May I call you Phoebe?"

And what if she said no?

"Come for a moment." He took her elbow and steered her into a corner of the room. He let go and pulled his mask down under his chin. His sandy hair thinned out above a heavy brow. His nose was forward, his chin strong and his ears battened down to the sides of his head, all in all a prow of a face, but what Phoebe noticed most when he took down his mask was that he smiled the smile of a man who had everything in hand. Including her. Or so he thought.

His deep-set eyes bored into her. "What is your opinion of Sister Kenny?"

She lowered her mask. "She's the one you made fun of on rounds?"

He paused without breaking his stare. "Doesn't pay to be touchy around here. But you must have an opinion about her. Don't worry about Dr. Sternberg, the old goat. I'll not tell any tales." He flashed her a charming grin around perfectly even teeth.

"I don't. I mean I don't know anything about her. Should I?"

"Quite interesting theories and she's had some marvelous success. She doesn't believe in all our casting and splinting, claims it impedes the return of function. Dr. Sternberg is all exercised because she's been in the States this past year to spread her gospel. He won't be schooled by a nurse. Rather silly, don't you think?"

She gave him a small, ambiguous shrug.

His hand was so quick, she had no time at all to dodge his sudden hummingbird touch, two soft taps of a fingertip on her temple. "You've got a brain in there, Phoebe. Don't let the likes of Dr. Sternberg bully you out of using it. Tell you what, I'll bring you some articles about Sister Kenny's *quackery*." He laughed and just like that he was gone, leaving a spot which tingled where he'd touched her.

She Holds the Face of the World

Amanda Sledz

Kali-Ma
(On Working for an Assault Hotline in the Appalachian Hills)

Woman says:

"Walked in on my boyfriend. He was with my four-year-old daughter. He was touching her all kinds of places. Called the police, and they can't find him, but I know where he is. I'm gonna kill him."

She says: "I know what they'll put her through. First they'll give her this exam and stick objects she doesn't understand in places she no longer loves to collect DNA on swabs they'll probably lose. Then they'll put her on a stand and give her a doll and ask her to show the court what happened. Say, 'Did he use his thing? His private parts?' And she'll look scared and confused, and the defense will call her an 'unreliable witness' and that's when they'll call me up."

"And I'll tell them what I saw, and they'll say, 'You was angry at the defendant, wasn't you?' They'll say maybe he was gonna break up with me. Maybe I threatened him. I'll say 'I don't know about that, all I know is he smelled like dead man the minute he sunk his dick into my daughter. He smelled like gunpowder.'"

"And they'll say, 'Is that a threat?' and they'll pack that man in a bulletproof vest so I don't do what needs doing—and we both know what needs doing."

She says: "Am I wrong for thinking this?"

And I respond: "No. Where is your daughter? Is she safe now?"

She says: "She's sitting on my lap. I told her she needs to go to her Nana's for a little while. Just a little while. She doesn't want me to go. But I'm fixin' to have myself a little accident, if you know what I mean."

I do. People have accidents all the time. Hell, just recently in Athens County a certain pedophile ate the wrong batch of brownies. He just so happened to die.

Then she asks me: "What would you do?"

And I say: "I'd hide the body."

She laughs, and so do I, because neither of us wants to believe I'm serious. So I add with the new accent infecting my tongue: "I don't rightly know."

I want to tell her: There are children who don't remember, or wash it cleaner in their minds. Transform it into a less-fulfilling game of doctor. Some people become scientists anyway, end up okay anyway. Some people do, anyway.

Instead: I spin tales of trusting the system, of the wonders of counseling. I congratulate her for electing not to continue to share a bed with unfortunate company, for not considering her four-year-old a hussy, like some might.

She says: "I don't know about those women. I just know about this one. I'm her mother. And I know where he is."

Susan Russell

How I Learned to Rap in Jail

Built almost entirely of cinderblocks, the Juvenile Justice Center in Portland, Oregon, is your average contemporary detention facility. It tentacles out from Central Control through a series of steel-bolted passageways, housing teens in a number of self-contained modules. The only artistic touch to the place is a string of statues at the main entranceway: rods of steel twisted into faceless human forms then welded onto park benches.

I'd passed these statues many times before in my work as a public defender but never paid much attention to them. Tonight I was here not as an attorney, but as a volunteer leading a creative writing workshop, and it was hard not to notice. Now as I looked at the faceless sculptures, I couldn't help but wonder—what chance did creativity have in a setting like this?

I pushed the intercom button in the lobby. "Can I help you?" a female voice asked.

"I'm here to facilitate a writing workshop in Bravo Two," I said. This was the module where boys, ages fifteen to seventeen, were housed while awaiting trial under Oregon's mandatory sentencing law, Measure 11. This law placed youth in adult court on serious charges and handed out stiff sentences for first-time offenders.

With notebooks in hand, I walked on, through tunneled hallways and locked doors. Every time the magnetic bolts snapped, I jumped. The sound, though expected, was too loud, too sudden; with each door, there was less chance of turning back. For the next ten weeks, I would be coming here to work with kids on writing. I was convinced if there was one thing that could have made a difference for me, with my chronic bad grades and repeated suspensions at school, it would have been a creative writing workshop. So I pressed on, hoping the jolt of the steel doors would soon wear off.

Lee, the staff leader on Bravo Two, greeted me at the door. He was a soft-spoken man with a stocking cap and a long gray ponytail. The workshop had been arranged over a month ago but somehow the boys had only just been informed and they weren't too happy. The workshop was meeting during their free time and it was a night for visitors and family calls.

"You couldn't have picked a worse time," Lee said. "It's partly my fault. I don't check my e-mails. If I'd known, I could have gotten them psyched for it."

The boys were in their rooms, which consisted of individual locked cells in two tiers that swept across the back wall and opened onto a broad communal area where they ate their meals, attended meetings, and hung out. If they weren't in their cells or the adjoining classroom, this is where they spent their time. A stoplight on the wall shone green. *Bravo 2 has been on green light for 83 days*, it read, a sign of good behavior. A rack of pencils hung nearby; for safety reasons, these weren't allowed in their rooms.

The kids peered through the windows of their cell doors. They looked out, then retreated, and then looked out again, waiting for the moment of release. The place smelled strange, an odd mixture of sweat, pine cleaner, and pizza.

"And the letters that were sent?" I asked Lee. Everything had been so well-planned, including letters outlining the workshop and inviting each boy to attend.

"Letters?" They had never made it into the boys' hands. "We need to do a better job coordinating between shifts."

The bottom line was that everything had changed. Rather than the six or so motivated participants I was expecting, the entire group—all sixteen—would be participating in the workshop. It wasn't mandatory, exactly. The boys had the option of spending the two hours locked in their cells instead.

"Ready to meet them?" Lee asked. "They're not a bad bunch." He was standing in the control room, a small glassed-in area with enough buttons and cameras to land a fleet of airplanes.

Lee pushed a master button and spoke directly into each cell, announcing my arrival. With another metallic buzz, the boys flooded out. They were dressed in matching tan pants and plain white tee shirts, pink socks, and plastic flip-flops.

They glanced at me sideways but when I caught their eyes, they turned away. Only one boy didn't look at me. He stared elsewhere and carried on talking to the other boys about how the workshop was stupid and he didn't want anything to do with it.

On command the boys went down the line, reciting their names, so many names, how would I remember them all? I hadn't been given a list. I would have to rely on memory and of course there would be turnover—new boys coming, others leaving—as their criminal charges were resolved.

She Holds the Face of the World

I scribbled down names as best I could: Latif, Rogelio, Jessie, Deondraye. The boy who wouldn't look at me was named Rashaud. Out of sixteen kids, ten were African-American, four Hispanic, and only two Caucasian, in a city that was more than 80 percent white.

"They're all yours," Lee said as he returned to his work station.

I needed to dazzle them with my introduction, take the bull by the horns, and pull hard. My name, my role. "I'm not a teacher, a volunteer. I'm just here to make sure the workshop runs smoothly."

I explained the program, how for the last eight years Write Around Portland had sponsored more than 250 volunteer-facilitated workshops for people who, because of income, isolation, or other barriers, might not have access to writing. I rattled off a list of other workshops: survivors of domestic violence, seniors in foster care, adults with disabilities, teenagers in drug and alcohol recovery, low-income adults.

"We publish an anthology each term, a book of the participants' writings." I held up a past issue. "Everyone gets to have a piece in it. At the end there's a release party and people read their work."

By now we were seated at three fixed tables with seats that swiveled in a circle.

The boys had begun to talk loudly, flipping each other off.

My chest tightened. How was this going to work? It seemed impossible to win them over.

"It's all about the writing," I continued as I passed out pens and journals—tan journals, no red or blue gang colors, and with no numbers that could be turned into gang signs. The pens were labeled and numbered; they would need to be collected at the end of each workshop. The jail was making a special exception letting the group write in ink.

The boys examined the notebooks with disinterest, uncapping the pens. Some began to doodle. They looked as if by ignoring me, they could make me go away.

"Who wants to be part of this writing workshop," I asked, "and who's here because it beats being locked in your cell?"

Now I had their attention. Two boys slowly raised their arms. They were sort of interested in the workshop. Rashaud had his back turned away as if he intended to lead the rest by example. He was tall, thin, and strikingly handsome. It was clear from the way he carried himself—his determined gestures and strong voice—that the other boys looked up to him.

I tossed out a warm-up assignment. "Write five things about yourself, four that are true and one that's false, then we'll guess which one's not true."

Some wrote but most continued to talk. When it came time to guess, they quickly sorted things out. They knew Chris didn't have five sisters and James didn't own a dog and Deondraye wasn't in here for a crime he didn't commit. The whole exercise lasted fifteen minutes. One hour, forty-five minutes to go. Several conversations were taking place now. At table two the boys had started to rap.

I handed out an excerpt from a novel, a female adult writing as a male child, a lesson on voice, how you can write as someone you're not, make stuff up, change endings to make them better or worse. Jessie volunteered to read the piece.

The piece was "okay," Deondraye said. I was surprised he could hear it above the rapping at table two. "All I have in this world is a pistol and a promise / A fist full of dollars, a list full of problems."[1]

"So you guys like rap?" I asked the group.

A few nodded. The rest shrugged. The answer was so obvious.

Rashaud turned around. He looked directly at me but only to roll his eyes.

"What is it you like about rap," I asked, "the words or the music?"

"Both," someone said.

"Why the words?" I asked. "Isn't the music enough?"

"The words tell the story, what the rap's about."

"Anybody here write rap?"

A few hands went up.

"Anybody here want to write rap?"

More hands.

She Holds the Face of the World

"Rap is writing," I told them. "We can write rap in this workshop if you want. It's up to you what we do. You make the rules."

The group was silent. They thought about this for a moment. Rap sounded like a good idea.

What part of rap did they want to work on first?

"Metaphor and simile," Rashaud answered. He was no longer looking away.

I asked him to define these terms in case the others didn't know. His answer would have floored any English teacher, a definition straight out of *Webster's*. Metaphor: a word or phrase used to suggest likeness. Simile: a comparison of unlike things.

"A good rap uses both metaphor and simile," Rashaud explained. He gave an example from "California Love": *"Now let me welcome everybody to the wild, wild west / A state that's untouchable like Elliot Ness."*[2]

Another boy continued the rap. *"The track hits ya eardrum like a slug to ya chest / Pack a vest for your Jimmy in the city of sex."*

I ripped out blank pages from my notebook and passed these around, promising to bring in lyrics as well as more traditional pieces. They took some time writing down rap artists whose work they wanted to read and handed these pages to me.

Then we worked together to make a list of group rules: If you're going to participate, you have to participate; stay focused; show respect; no side talking if it's disruptive; no cross tabling if it's disruptive; what's said in the group stays in the group. I added Write Around Portland's mandatory rule: No hate speech.

I finished with a free write. They could write whatever they wanted or respond to a prompt: "What you need to know about me is . . ."

Only a few wrote and nobody shared what they put down. Most were busy talking about rap and which songs they liked best.

I decided to quit while I was ahead. "Rap," I said. "Got it."

"See you next week," one of the boys said and waved.

On my way out the locked bolts didn't sound so loud; my mind was focused on the challenge that lay ahead, building a workshop around rap.

At home I looked more carefully at the lists the kids had made. I counted fifty or more artists. Easy-E, Lil Wayne, Three 6 Mafia, Mac Dre, BG, Babyface Assassins, Messy Marv. I only recognized one name: Tupac Shakur.

What I did know about rap was that it had gotten a bad reputation, the words were perceived as too graphic, too violent, with misogynist undertones and profanity. CDs came with parental advisory warnings and hit songs were dubbed for radio.

I found lyrics online—not too violent, not too extreme—and printed two versions, one edited, one not. Then I hesitated. I wouldn't be editing words from a literary passage so why was I doing this with lyrics? Surely the words were just as important to a song's message as they were to a novel or short story. I decided again to defer to the kids. *You make the rules*, I had told them.

"What do you guys think about sanitized lyrics?" I asked at the beginning of the next workshop.

"It's better to read the words the way they're written," Latif answered. "They're part of the rap. Besides, it's not like we don't know what they say when you blank them out."

"And the N-word?" I asked.

Sometimes the N-word was offensive, they explained, sometimes it was used to give power. It all depended on the context and who was using it. Their rule addressed this concern: When reading aloud only African-American kids could say it, the rest should just use N.

I passed out lyrics and we analyzed these, how Dr. Dre used lots of metaphor but Tupac was real and they liked this better. He was telling stuff that happened in his life and because of this it had more impact:

> *Black male slippin in hail when will we prevail*
> *Fearin jail but crack sales got me living well*
> *And the system's suicidal with this Thug's Life*
> *Stayin strapped forever trapped in this drug life.*[3]

They called out a list of ideas for a rap: snitches, freedom, streets, high times / good times, girls, drugs, money, guns. The kids began to write.

We read other works besides rap, like Sandra Cisnero's short story "Salvador Late or Early," about a boy with a hard life looking after his younger brothers. This time everyone stayed focused and the writing was transformed. Each time Salvador's name was read (and it appeared many times), the boys repeated this as a group and the reading took on a rap beat to which the piece naturally lent itself.

There were three rap stars they liked most of all: Mac Dre (not Dr. Dre), Tupac, and Lil Wayne. Only Lil Wayne was still alive. The other two had died of gunshot wounds. We read their writing, not just their lyrics. I even handed out Tupac's handwritten poetry from junior high and plays he wrote in prison. He wrote only one song in jail but twenty in two weeks once he was released. "So that's when it all came out," he wrote. "Freedom, Inspiration."[4]

Rashaud handled the photocopied pages like they were a rare manuscript. "This is his handwriting," he told the other boys. "This is what he actually wrote." He studied the pages during the workshop and I could tell he would read them again (and again) after we finished for the night.

After four weeks, the boys began to open up. We no longer sat on fixed seats at separate tables but on plastic chairs in a round circle. Some wrote rap, others poetry and prose. I tried my hand at a rap: *"This beat's got me goin' / It's inside my head / Follow the groove where it takes me / No fear where I tread."*

"Keep working it," Latif suggested. "You might have something there."

More kids joined us including Sam, who was fifteen but seemed much younger thanks to the pageboy haircut his sister gave him before he came to detention. He wrote poems about innocence, *love means happiness*, and took on the role of handing out pens. New Latino kids added music to our list: Brownside and South Park Mexicans. Latif, the most prolific rapper, explained how things worked to the new kids and gave a positive critique—"not too bad"—to a sixteen-year-old white boy who wrote rap for the first time.

"I've recorded a bit," Latif told me. "I pretty much got a contract when I get out."

The boys thrived on positive feedback. Each week I sent them post cards, standard fare for Write Around Portland, colorful cards with strong messages, *Poetry must be made by all and not one*, and a handwritten personal note: *I loved your piece about . . . Your writing is great . . . Thanks for being part of the group.* Sam put his cards up in his room and told me what colors he needed to make the rainbow on his wall complete. Rashaud acknowledged them, too. It was the only mail he got, other than from his lawyer.

Rashaud no longer sat as far away from me as possible. His rap lyrics began to talk about what it felt like being locked up and how he struggled to make it through bad times, but still it was pretty hard. He read his lyrics to canned beats from the computer— "they call me lil brezz but I been snatched the lil"—and asked for pictures of his favorite rap stars to cut out and tape on his journal. He was marking his notebook with artists he admired, and filling it with his own writing, as were the others. Each week I brought in a new supply.

Kids came, kids left. Each time, I said goodbye to Rashaud with a feeling of sadness and loss only to find out his trial date had been postponed, yet again, and he was still part of the group. He waved with excitement when he saw me then quickly lowered his eyes.

I felt like Wendy from *Peter Pan* and these were my lost boys. I was darning their clothes but there were too many holes and I didn't have enough thread. I wanted to turn back the clock to a time when the holes weren't so big. Could a workshop like this have made a difference?

Now when I was alone in my car, I found myself listening and singing to rap music, the loud beat setting the pace of my driving. At work, I was more lighthearted, less bogged down by the hopelessness of the system. I was witnessing firsthand how much these kids had to offer when given a chance on their own terms. I wasn't naïve enough to believe everything had changed but still I imagined a different life for my clients—adults charged with federal crimes—had they been given this same opportunity when they were young. I prided myself on bringing hope and respect to my clients, encouraging them to believe in themselves no matter how bad things seemed. Now I expanded this. "Have you thought about keeping a journal?" I asked. "Maybe it would help."

As we wrote together, I learned more about the boys' stories, how many were in on robbery charges and how Latif had been shot three times but still liked guns. I learned that Rashaud was charged with an act of violence against a stranger and I was able to connect the dots—an abusive father, his mother's blind eye, Rashaud's anger at the system. I learned how young sweet Sam, always trying so hard to please, was facing a twenty-five-year sentence even though he had no criminal history. I knew as a lawyer this could mean only one thing, sexual contact with someone under twelve. Not forceable contact, that wasn't part of the crime. I pictured Sam seeking comfort from his own abuse in the arms of a younger cousin or neighbor.

"Only in this state would he be charged," his lawyer told me when he called to ask for a letter of recommendation for Sam.

We had come full circle from juvenile courts with individualized attention and treatment. Now these courts were being jettisoned in favor of a get-tough-on-crime approach, despite the studies showing that long sentences only increased recidivism.

I wrote to Sam's attorney, describing Sam's immaturity and his need for counseling, not jail.

The workshop moved into its final weeks and I watched the boys soften, their emotions develop, as they let down their guard and revealed parts of themselves that others rarely saw: Rashaud with his guarded mistrust; Latif who knew how to work the system; Sam with his emotional needs that seemed almost endless. The boys worked hard on their final pieces and shared these in the group. We held our own release party, complete with pizza and soda. Few would be out of jail in time for the anthology's official launch.

The boys read their pieces aloud to resounding rounds of applause. Deondraye's piece was about hope and believing in yourself. Rogelio wrote about the light at the end of the tunnel. Rashaud about how he wished he could go back in time, though he knew he would make the same mistakes again. Sam's story was about love and family. Wayne wrote that having your father's name isn't a gift at all, not if you don't know your father: "At night I say I love you and hear no response." Chris's rap, "Bein' behind Bars," was intricate, about how much you lose when you're young and locked up. Latif named his piece, "NEGLIGENCE."

As the workshop came to an end, the boys asked if I could stay a bit longer. Latif suggested I organize a workshop at the long-term facility where most of them were headed. He had his agenda, to become a rap star, and was thinking of ways to keep working on his writing. Sam, too, was moving on, forming new relationships with other teachers and guards. And Rashaud? Making connections with adults wasn't easy for him but he had made one here with me. "Best ever," he wrote in his evaluation, which he turned in only after he made sure nobody else was around. How would this relationship help him in the future? I wouldn't see any of the boys again; our time together had ended. Surely something Rashaud had learned about trust and respect would carry with him into the future.

We finished the workshop where we began, talking about the power of writing and the chance it gave them to tell their stories. I wasn't the first to say this of course. Tupac, in a rap interlude, had made this clear before:

The Last Poets did it with poetry...
even in our history
from ancient African civilization
Poets went from village to village

And that's how stories and messages and lessons were taught...

We picked it up, we picked up those positive vibes...
And we started rappin... [5]

Notes
1. Lil Wayne. "Carter II." Lyrics. *Carter II*. Cash Money, 2005.
2. Shakur, Tupac featuring Dr. Dre and Roger Troutman. "California Love (Remix)." *All Eyez on Me*. Death Row, 1996.
3. Shakur, Tupac. "My Block (Remix)." *Better Dayz*. Amaru/Death Row, 2002.
4. Shakur, Tupac. *Resurrection*. New York: Atria, 2003.
5. Shakur, Tupac. "Interlude." Lyrics. *The Rose that Grew from Concrete*. Amaru/ Interscope, 2000.

Julie Rogers

Wisdom Tree

We sat in mock night, the shades drawn, staring up at the flickering screen that projected driving simulations: clean cars very carefully and mindfully winding their way through wide streets of manicured neighborhoods. It was Friday afternoon and Drivers Ed was the last class of the day. Our limbs pressed together, knees bumping up against the metal legs of our desks and chairs, we squirmed and sweated in the cramped portable waiting for the weekend to begin. We'd had enough of fake driving. Our sixteen-year-old bodies itched to get behind the wheel, to feel the hard resin beneath our fingers, the stiff pedal beneath our toes, to launch ourselves into freedom.

Our teacher, Coach Parker, never shifted his gaze from the screen—the images refracted through his enormous metal-rimmed glasses with lenses so thick they made his eyes look three times their actual size. His bald head was so closely shaven, we could actually watch the film reflected on its shiny, smooth surface. Coach was most likely a former military man and cut a striking figure. Strong and taut, he was always neatly dressed in fitted trousers and short-sleeved, button-down shirts with a pocket on the left. He was much beloved by the school's athletes, but his stern approach intimidated and alienated those of us disposed to less active pursuits.

So, when he suddenly turned those mantis eyes on the back row and said rather loudly, "Do you two have something to say?" we were all drawn out of our stupor.

Joe Bettis and Andy Planck were being as they always were—stupid and loud and feeding off each other's inability to sit still. We all groaned because we knew only too well what was coming next.

"You two can't pay attention and I see a lot of sleepy eyes in here, so I guess you know what time it is," said Coach. "Well?"

"It's time for a visit to the Wisdom Tree," a few students in the front row murmured.

"What's that? I can't hear you!"

"The Wisdom Tree!" we all shouted so we wouldn't be asked again.

"That's right, people! Let's move it!"

Coach turned off the projector, opened the door and blew his whistle. We stumbled from the trailer, single-file, eyes painfully squinted against the sun. We did as Coach had instructed months ago during our first class: "Run up the stairs, do a lap around the front of the school, touch it and give thanks!"

The Wisdom Tree. It was a young maple—the diameter of its trunk no bigger than that of a basketball's and its tallest branch no higher than the roof of the single story school. Because the tree was neither old nor impressive in its reach to the heavens, we were perplexed as to why Coach believed there was even a hint of wisdom to be had by slapping its dull bark. His near mystical relationship with what seemed to us no more than a sapling was bewildering. One by one we were made to jog beneath its scant canopy, lay our hands on the object of our scorn, and give it thanks before quickly returning to our makeshift classroom. We found this exercise neither inspiring nor heart-warming on a Friday afternoon, summer just starting to make an appearance, and the sound of car keys tickling the brain. We'd tapped the Wisdom Tree countless times, felt the injustice and indignation of it all, but soon we'd be free.

The week before school let out, I went four-wheeling with my friend Amy and her boyfriend, James, who was two years older than we were. He had an old Jeep and a case of beer and he took us up into the hills that surrounded our town. We sat looking out over the woods to the bay and the San Juan Islands beyond as we drank our beer.

"I hate my new house," said Amy, whose parents had just built a home miles from town. "How am I supposed to get anywhere? They built that house just to keep me from having a life. Like Greg's party last weekend. I couldn't get a ride and ... hey, how was it? What did I miss?"

I could barely remember the party but fragmented images passed through my mind like a slide show of shame: too much to drink, Greg, the sad drunken ride home, slipping into my house without waking my mother. "Oh, you know, the usual crowd, the usual beer, the music. It's always the same. I can't wait to be done with this school."

The more we drank, the more worked up we got about our many teen grievances: our parents and their fighting and their stupid curfews; friends we no longer liked because they'd become stuck up; the neighbors who spied on us when our parents were at work and ratted us out; and, of course, school. We couldn't stand the office lady who wouldn't accept our forged late slips; the counselors who were never there when you had a problem, but who were great at chiding you for bad behavior; Coach and his damn tree.

"I swear to God, one of these days I'm going to cut that fucking tree down."

The enormity of Amy's words hung there above the three of us. Something in her tone let us know she wasn't fooling around. We sat silently looking at each other and it was obvious we'd all had the same thought many times, but none had dared speak it.

"Let's do it. Tonight," Amy finally said.

We both turned to James. "I have an axe in the back." He motioned to the jeep with a shrug.

With the sun low in the sky, we barreled down the mountain at perilous speeds, spinning mud and gravel, nearly toppling over several times but laughing at the danger. Beer in the veins and risk on the horizon. Back in town, James got us some more beer and we sat in a field near the school waiting for the sky to darken. I'd blown my curfew again.

Just after midnight, we parked behind the school and walked around to the front, giggling nervously and scoping out the scene. The school's entrance was lit by a few flood lights so the tree was not in total darkness as I'd imagined. Its spindly frame cast a sharp thin shadow against the lawn and, for a moment, something akin to pity washed over me; but the fear of getting caught quickly made a prisoner of my thoughts. We'd have to move fast.

James drew his axe back and landed the first blow with a muted "thud," barely making a chip in the thin bark. The blade was dull. "Shit!" was all he said before hacking maniacally at the base, sweat pouring off his nose and chin. Amy and I kept looking up toward the road, knowing the cops made their rounds all through the night.

The crack of the axe against the moist pulp reverberated off the walls and down the exterior corridors of the school. "Someone's going to hear this. C'mon, James! God, I can't believe we're doing this!" Amy was both panicked and laughing hysterically. I knew how she felt though I stood in dumb, paralytic stillness watching the massacre, watching the road, back and forth, until it was all over. It took over half an hour to fell the Wisdom Tree.

On Monday morning an announcement went out over the loud speaker: There would be an afternoon assembly to discuss the vandalism that had occurred over the weekend. Attendance mandatory. The day stretched out before me like a piece of taffy, each tick of the clock's second hand caught in its sticky sweetness. I found myself panting in the girls' bathroom, my head hung over the sink, unable to shake the vision of the small tree as it stood, just before joining its shadow in the grass. I stayed clear of Amy.

The atmosphere in the gym was electric. A low rumble started up as Coach, microphone in hand, just stood there, tears slowly rolling down his face.

"We love you, Coach!" some of the girls' basketball team shouted and, as the power of the collective took hold, a low rumble mounted. "Yeah, Coach, we love you," from what seemed like most of the student body.

Finally able to speak, Coach started his booming voice, "As you all by now know, over this past weekend, someone came onto school property and chopped down..." and here he had to pause. "The Wisdom Tree was a symbol. A reminder that sometimes we get too caught up in our thoughts, feelings and problems and, when that happens, we need to go and touch something real, something that's rooted and that connects us to nature, which passes no judgment."

"And so, I believe the person, or persons who did this were caught up in their own petty thoughts and feelings and perhaps felt powerless against them and that's why they did this thing. Because this was an act of weakness. Weakness of character and spirit. Whoever's responsible for this, please come forward. Naturally, there will be consequences but, if you come clean now, you might actually be able to start forgiving yourself because believe me, someday—maybe today, maybe tomorrow or even many years from now—you will regret what you've done."

Going to Drivers Ed class after that speech was like being dragged to the gallows. I was sweating and couldn't stop shaking. I was convinced that Coach, with his magnifying lenses for eyes, would be able to see right through me. But when I got to class, he was distant and didn't make a lot of eye contact with anyone. He spoke a bit about class certificates and what to expect on the state driving test. He told us we'd been good students and that he was excited for us to start this new chapter in our lives as drivers. But before he released us for the day, he rather quietly and somberly said, "There's one thing I want you to do before you head out for the day. C'mon, people, let's go."

And so we marched up and out to the lawn and, without having to be asked, one by one bent down and touched what remained of the Wisdom Tree and whispered, "Thank you."

Summer came and went and Amy and I slowly drifted apart. I simply found it difficult to look at her, though I blamed her for nothing and none of us ever confessed. Shame is a capricious bedfellow. Eventually, I left our small town and have since lived in far-flung cities, suburbia, and the quiet of the country, moving frequently, restless and eager for a fresh start. Rootless.

But now that I have daughters of my own, I've settled into a house in an old neighborhood where the streets are lined with ancient trees whose branches form archways the residents drive and walk under. In front of my house stands a dark-leafed tree where my husband has hung a swing for my daughters. As summer begins to show itself, I watch my girls sway back and forth and, though the bough sighs and creaks under their weight, I trust that it will hold. I know how strong a tree can be.

Crista Cornelius

Running with Dragons

You know it's been raining all night because you frequently woke to the sound of water clattering on your roof and the wind splashing it against the side of the house like an aggressive housekeeper whipping the dirt out of her rugs. When you heard this in the dark of night and during the gloomy suggestion of dawn, you smiled, breathed in the clean, wet scent, and snuggled deeper into your flannel sheets. You didn't wonder about your daily morning jog, fret about whether or not to go out there and face all that. Instead, you smiled a little more at the thought.

Morning light finally arrives. You ponder briefly about what to wear, then grab the usual: decades-old sweatpants, a tee shirt from the half-marathon you limped one spring, wool socks, ball cap with knit cap over it, running shoes, and your old black coat. You open the front door and leaves rush forward like determined protesters. You usher them back out but express your appreciation for their efforts and the way the sheen of rain enhances their gold and maroon colors.

Without hesitation, you're out on the sidewalk, doing your jog-trot and smiling broadly in spite of raindrops so thick you feel as if you're breathing underwater. No one else is out. It's an empty movie set. Then, a bike-commuter whizzes by, but his expression is the opposite of yours: grit, determination, and a little pissed. If you're going to be out in it, you think, you may as well embrace it.

Most mornings, you do not feel like this. Instead, you labor over tying your shoes, just to delay the run, your first effort of a long day ahead. Usually, you battle dread and anxiety, but not today. Today, you think of the poet Rilke who wrote about dragons—his metaphor for fear and despair. He believed fighting your dragons, putting your energy into resisting them, only makes them more powerful. Rilke advises that you accept their existence, accept the dread and anxiety. Today, you try not to think much about dragons at all, try not to notice them bearing down. Today, you let the rain's relentless abundance consume your attention.

At first you jog delicately, sidestepping puddles. After a few blocks, you encounter the first flooded intersection. Debris clogs sewage drains, making them completely invisible in the foot-deep mini-pond. You find a route around. Even so, as soon as you're back on the sidewalk, perky yellow leaves mask a small but deep puddle. Your right foot sinks in, soaking wool sock and dousing the leg of your sweatpants so thoroughly, the weight of the rainwater drags the waistband downward, threatening to tug the pants right off. By the second flooded intersection, where an SUV crawls through but still expels waves of water waist high, you dive right in. Why not? You're soaked already. Your socks weigh about three pounds each. Your old coat no longer lives up to its water-resistant label and is like the lush at the bar, avidly soaking up every last drop and looking for more.

By now, you're ecstatic. It's November but almost warm outside and the rain is thick, soft, and silky. Branches have crashed all over sidewalks and into the streets in the night. You leap over them like a cat, like a fat cat anchored down by extra pounds of matted fur. You don't think to worry about more branches crashing down on your head. This won't happen to you. You're part of the scene, part of this storm. The trees seem to know that. In fact, you're so sure the trees know it, you leap up to high-five a crimson-leafed cherry tree which shimmers in response.

A silver haze curtains the wide, empty avenues. A jogger dressed in black comes into focus, running toward you down the middle of the street, only the second person you've seen in this post-apocalyptic rain. You prepare a smile, consider leaping out from the sidewalk to embrace her, to acknowledge: "We're here! You and me, out in this! No one else." Obviously you're sisters. But as she nears and you beam your dripping smile, she stays focused forward, eyes on the ground, frowning and furious. This almost makes you sad, reminds you of your dragons, so after she passes, you hip-bump a hedge and deliberately leap into a puddle next to someone's driveway.

Nevertheless, the dragons are right behind you, beside you, in front of you. Rilke suggests that no matter what burden they lean onto your shoulders or what ache they burn in your clenched stomach, a calm, steady gaze will unveil their disguise and reveal the scaly beasts to be princesses, princesses "who are only waiting to see us act, just once, with beauty and courage." You want to act with beauty and courage, not just once, but all the time. Leaping into puddles feels a little bit beautiful and somewhat courageous. You squint through the rain, try to eye your dragons squarely.

More branches cover sidewalks and streets. Rain, you realize, has the power to float houses, cities, and countries right off the map. Rain feeds toxic molds and mildews. And yet, that seems like a different kind of rain. An angry rain. Not today's rain that mutes all sound but its own.

Soon, you're home, more wet than if you'd stepped into the shower fully clothed. You stand on the doormat inside, strip off your hat, coat, and sweatpants. Your wet wool socks mop shiny footprints everywhere you step on the wood floor. You wrap a blanket around your bare legs and sit down to write.

Sometimes it's a day to stay in, to find your favorite blanket, a library book, a cup of tea, and wait it out. Sometimes it's a day to open the front door and step right into it, embrace it unconditionally, stubbornly refuse to be blown off course. A day to strive for beauty and courage. To see if a kind, steady gaze will unveil the princess hiding inside the dragon. To see if Rilke had it right: that the things that scare us are, in their deepest essence, things that want our love. Today was that kind of day.

Two

Heidi Beierle

Carnage

Ten bike-lengths up ahead, a brown lump rests on the fog line of the shoulderless highway. If it's scat, I'd put money on bear.

I'm a lone female pedaling through southwestern Montana—the Ruby Valley, named for abundant garnets. It's bear country and I'm heading toward West Yellowstone. July. Bears are hungry, not ravenous, right?

Scat isn't one of those things that typically prompts me to stop. If a slow approach reveals something compelling—shape, odor, contents, signature—only then will I get off and look.

It could be man-made, a work glove or knit hat.

The lump doesn't hold a solid edge like a pile of scat—it wavers ever so slightly. Closer still, crisp lines. Road kill. I'm excited, as if this dead animal were a longed-for birthday present. I unclip from my pedals, stand straddling my bike and look down at tidy, chocolate-colored feathers. Long black eyelashes set against a white face-blaze as if it were napping. The little beak, curved into the road, the color of the road. Posed like me when I take a nap, belly down, head turned to the side, wings folded, feathers spread out like a blanket. A slight breeze raises some feathers on its back; they flap noiselessly back into place.

I take a picture from above, then take another with my mind's eye, clip in and continue.

How did it die? No one better drive over it and crush it.

I turn around and come back up to it. This time, I dismount from my bike and lay it down on the embankment. Three male cyclists loaded with touring gear stop on the other side of the road.

"Do you need help?" one of them asks.

"No thanks," I say. We talk across the road. "There's this little owl. It doesn't seem right to let it get squashed on the road. I'm going to move it." To my relief, the cyclists continue and I turn to the owl.

I don't often find owls dead on the road, and it isn't simply that they become husk and chaff. Feathers don't stick to the road—they still try to lift off when cars pass.

Does the spirit stay connected? When a car drives over the physical trace, is the spirit brutalized, does it feel crush and tread mark again and again? Just thinking about the owl getting crunched triggers a muscular lurch through my torso that starts deep in my pelvis and ends in my esophagus. Four years back, when I was biking to work, I cut the crossing too close: three lanes of cars, mad engines accelerating. I was depressed, already felt dead, had thrown away everything precious. Nothing mattered.

In that instant, in front of the cars, the assumed impact entered my right side, knee ripped sideways, leg breaking at the femur, rib cage collapsing and the broken bones piercing my lungs, liver, and heart, blood flooding my insides, head hitting the road, and blackness.

On the other side of the intersection, I didn't know what had just happened—or hadn't happened. I thought I was dead. I looked to the street behind me for a clue, something to ground me. I didn't see myself a bloody splatter on the road or my bike a knot of metal, just the cars rushing past. I continued pedaling, looked at my chest, arms, legs, feet, hands—same, same, same, same, same. I guessed I was alive.

I pick up the owl, fold its wings around its body, light and tiny in my cycling-gloved palms. The owl's head hangs forward, long neck hidden and weighted by its skull. I turn the owl over and hold it in my left hand, tracing with my fingertips the bones along its left wing, then the right. The wing bends between elbow and wrist where it should be strong and rigid, the bone crushed like eggshell. I slide my fingers down the brief slope of the owl's beak, touch the tawny feathers on its breast, so soft I can't feel them, then its feet. The tiny talons, black daggers, the toes that hold them, yellow, dainty and gecko-like, their undersides minutely dimpled and rough-looking, sticking out from sandy bloomers. I take up a toe between thumb and index finger, the talon, smooth and warm with a sharp point, like a cat's claw.

I step down the embankment and lay the owl on curled dead leaves at a plant's base.

Let a coyote run off with it, let microbes eat it molecular mouthful by molecular mouthful. Give the spirit a chance to gently disengage, like a spider web pulled down one anchor at a time.

I climb up the embankment, heft my bike back onto the road and journey on.

Every day, every moment, the owl's fate could be my own. I live and pedal in acknowledgment of this. I only hope that when death arrives, a radiant heart will free my feathers from the road.

Jackie Shannon Hollis

Left As It Was, It Would Come Apart

In a small town with a high school of just over a hundred kids it is possible to be many things. I was a popular girl, honor society president, an actor in every school play, the girl who friends came to with their problems. I was the dance team leader, a setter on the volleyball team, a princess at the prom, and I was a slut. I excelled.

The boys I would be with were the older ones, most of them already graduated from high school. They smoked pot and partied and knew things about cities and music and drugs and the world. Things I thought I should know, things I wanted to know. They asked me out. They took me for a drive. I didn't say no. Word got around.

Each time, with each new boy, there was that first urge and pull, the hot breathlessness of it, and the possibility that this boy could do for me what I did for myself when I was alone: bring pleasure and relief. There was the possibility he could give me love and I could give it to him and we could go on like that, romance and love, passion under the moonlight, in the backseat of a car. But this didn't happen. They were boys and they knew even less than I knew.

There were girls with serious boyfriends. Girls already planning to marry after high school, to stay in our small town, to start a family. This was not my plan. This was not my mother's plan. She'd been talking about college since the end of my sophomore year, talking about it like it was my idea, something that would happen, not a question. Talking about it long enough that I did think it was my idea. This is where my mother's attention was. She saw to it that I made it home by curfew, kept up with my grades, sports, plays, dance team, chores. She didn't know about the rest. All those boys. All those backseats.

One night I drove home from a party, whiskey and beer and cigarettes and boy on me. I drove the highway slow and careful and drunk, took the turnoff to our farm, up the gravel road, lights of the house ahead.

Mom would be awake as she was always awake, waiting for her family to come home. But the older kids were grown and gone. Cris was a child, already in bed. Dad was still out at the bar like he had been most nights for years while she waited, while I waited, we all waited. While we looked for his lights in the driveway, felt the disappointment when he finally came home, drunk and distant. She had stopped waiting for him. He would be home sometime. I was the one to wait for now, the only one Mom expected.

I parked in the driveway. Turned the engine off. Mom there in her chair in the lamp-lit picture window. TV flicker. I got out slow and careful, held myself on car door, hood of car. Steadied on the picket fence, the gate, deep whiskey breath, up the sidewalk, legs like bendy straws, up the porch steps.

I opened the front door and stood there, loose-eyed, sway in my legs. Mom had a pad of thick art paper on her lap, calligraphy pens spread out around her. Some old movie on the TV.

"Hi," I said, the thick drunk of it in my throat.

She looked at the clock. One a.m., right on time.

"Hi," she said. Her eyes up and down on me.

I started past her to go to the bathroom. My shoulder bumped the wall, and I caught myself there, looked to see if she saw. This was where Dad stood, all those nights when he finally came home, his dinner dried up in the oven, us kids on our way to bed.

Mom sat up straighter. "Are you drunk?"

He would ask us what we'd learned at school that day. Stand there, the top of him making small swaying circles. We gave one word answers, "Fine, okay, good," knowing he wouldn't remember in the morning.

I turned the rest of the way around, stood up tall. "No," I said to Mom, tried to hold my eyes steady on hers. Like that would prove it.

She didn't blink. "You are," she said.

"I am not," I said.

She looked back at the paper in front of her. "It's not good for a girl to get drunk." The careful lettering in black ink. Lines and swirls. "It's not ladylike." She said it like another mother-daughter talk. "You're just supposed to get a glow on. A drink or two," she said. "To feel happy. That's all. Otherwise it's sloppy. And ugly."

Her innocence floated in the air between us. I squinted at her. I used to think she could see through me. But she had no idea how much I drank, how many cigarettes I smoked, what that boy and I had just been doing in the backseat of my car. She picked up her pen. She drew slow inky lines on the thick paper and the paper took that ink in.

I felt a love for her then, warm in my face and chest, and a little sick, tight in my stomach, an ache. That she still believed in me. Believed I was good. That she could still teach me the ways to be a lady.

❖ ❖ ❖

A few months later, Mom smiled a quiet smile when I asked if she and Dad would be chaperones for the high school prom.

"I was voted princess," I said.

"Your dad will be tickled you asked." Her smile went bigger. "Me too."

For a moment, I imagined we were that kind of family, like the families of my friends who didn't have secrets to keep from their parents.

On the night before prom, I left the pink satin dress I'd made in Home Ec hanging on the coat closet door. The pattern was sexy, like an old-fashioned movie star, and the dress almost looked like that. It showed off my strong shoulders, my slim waist. But I'd made that dress with the opposite of the care I'd put into Dad's western shirt, last year's Home Ec project. I'd made the dress sloppy and fast and just to get it done.

The next morning Mom pointed at the dress. "I got to looking at your sewing on that. The seams were a little loose." She seemed proud when she told me she'd stayed up late, re-sewed every seam. "I was afraid it would come apart when you dance," she said. I felt ashamed. I felt angry. My poor work, her need to check it.

I'm sure I didn't thank her.

❖ ❖ ❖

My date and I wandered into the dance over an hour late, steps fluid with alcohol, eyes wide on speed. The pink satin dress was creased and the hem dirty with mud from the back road we'd been on, drinking and making out.

The crowning ceremony was over. Another girl wore the crown.

Mom and Dad stood at the back of the room, arms folded, eyes narrow. I fought the bad feeling in me, took my date's hand and went over to them. Like I could make up for it, the way I was embarrassing them in front of the other parents, the teachers, their own hope that I was a better girl. I said, "Oh, sorry. We lost track of time." And I laughed.

Their tight faces, mouths in straight lines holding words they wouldn't say because this was public and they wouldn't embarrass themselves any more than I already had.

I nudged Mom toward my date. "C'mon Mom, dance with him and I'll dance with Dad." Mom pulled at my arm. "Where were you?"

Dad ran his hand over his face and said to Mom, "Jeanie, we'll talk about this later." He was completely sober. "We don't want to dance," he said.

My date and I moved away. I stayed on the far side of the room, not looking their way, not wanting to feel that shame, how stupid I was, how thoughtless I was.

I stayed out until sunrise, putting off "later" as long as possible.

❖ ❖ ❖

The dawn light made shadows in the family room when I came in the front door.

"You're late."

I could see just the silhouette of Dad there in his chair.

I stayed by the door, my hand on the knob.

"I know."

I'd fallen asleep in the car with my date. That sexy satiny dress had done its job and it had held together, but now it was wadded up in the back seat. I wore old jeans and a tee shirt.

"Come here," he said.

His disappointment was like something I could touch. It made his eyes soft and his shoulders loose. It filled the air around him. I thought I might cry. He took my hand and pulled me down onto his lap. I hadn't been in his lap since I was a little girl. Faint memory of cupping my hands over the stubble on his chin, my head against his chest, my feet barely reaching his knees.

Now, I kept my body stiff and upright and awkward. My legs next to his, feet on the floor, his hand around my shoulder. Would he smell the sex on me, the cigarettes?

"You've gotten so grown up," he said. He put his arms around me and I relaxed, just a little. I leaned into him. For one sweet moment, I was his Brown-Eyed Girl again. It had been so long since either he or Mom had touched me or held me. And just for that moment, I felt his love and his loss, and mine. The old grandfather clock ticked, the shadows in the room faded. And then it felt awkward and false, me there on his lap.

I sat up and his arms loosened. He touched my chin, turning it so that our eyes met. "You embarrassed your mother tonight," he said. "I'm disappointed in you."

Some things are easier to know without the words. Hearing them out loud came with a weight. His disappointment. All those nights I'd waited for him to come home. I could have felt glad for him to know just a moment of what it was like, him drunk, me waiting. But he was the father. I was the daughter.

"Get your car keys," he said. "You're not driving that car for a week."

I almost laughed at the smallness of it, after what I'd done, after all I'd been doing. I stood up, stiff-backed. I went to my purse, found the keys and gave them to him. He nodded and put them in his pocket. "One week," he said.

I never even had to ask Mom or Dad for a ride, I never had to take the school bus. I never said I was sorry. My friends, or one of those boys, came to pick me up before school and dropped me off after, and the shame I felt at disappointing my parents faded in the dust of those cars coming up our gravel road, and I kept on with my wild ways.

I wish I still had that dress. I thought it was beautiful.

Karen Guth

Your Hand at Your Throat

That slice of scarlet. You adjust your scarf, feeling my gaze. I flick my eyes to your face then. So young. We hold hands across the table, mother and daughter, you for once not caring who sees it.

Outside the afternoon fades to dusk. The neon sign in the window flickers off and on, warming up. "Georg's" it flashes, missing the *e* as it has since this was my hangout too, back when I was about your age. Old George is long gone, but "Georg's" lives on among the students and professors here. They pour in from the cold, from the unrelenting grip of sub-zero weather that is Iowa in January. It's happy hour. Steam drifts from wet clothing and voices shout in greeting. "Gay-org!" A young man leans across the bar. "Set 'em up!" You grow anxious as you watch the door, but I squeeze your hands more tightly and tell you it'll be OK. Just watch for him.

You called me that night, called me from down in a deep dark place that no girl should ever be. Of course I came here as soon as I could, from half a continent away. The campus police had finished their investigation, had found nothing. "What were you wearing?" they asked you. I am incredulous still.

I try not to imagine how it was for you, but I can't help but imagine what will never be. Those first fleeting glances that grow into lingering looks that develop into whispered exchanges and maybe a first date for coffee, just to see, and then if that seems promising there may be dinner or a movie (do young people still date like that?) and afterward those first awkward, groping touches where the skin feels electrified upon contact and the world falls away and you find yourself in a place you never knew existed. It won't be. I so wanted that for you. Wouldn't every mother? Instead you will have fear, may never know love, won't trust enough for love. My throat tightens with the thought.

I feel your body stiffen across the table, and your hands squeeze mine so tightly it hurts. It hurts. I see him now, too. You would never know. He looks just like any of the other college boys in the bar. How could you have known? He orders a beer and turns around to see who else is there, blowing on his cold hands. Dark has descended outside and the bar is dim. He doesn't see us.

You and I don't really have a plan. Did we just need to see him? Just need to put the whole thing in some kind of perspective, with the hope that you could get past it? But seeing him creates a roiling in my gut that begins somewhere deep down and threatens to come up. My head pounds and a small bead of sweat trickles down the back of my neck. You sense my rage. "Don't," you say, strangely calm, but I am already on my feet and walking toward the bar. What propels me I can't say, but it is something outside of myself and conscious thought. It is visceral and primeval and it all happens in a flash, my belt around his neck, pulling, pulling. I am giddy with it, with him feeling your pain.

"Don't," you say again and I realize that I am still sitting here with you. It surprises me. It was so real, so disconcertingly real. You speak softly into your phone and then we wait. We wait through happy hour, mostly silent, our hands entwined. The boy is drunk now, and loud, and finally two policemen come in through the back door and you point to him on his barstool and they raise their eyebrows as if to say, "Him? Really?" and you nod. They grasp his arms from behind and twist them behind his back, yanking him off the stool. He stumbles as they half carry, half drag him through the back door to a waiting car. He still doesn't see us. Your face glows red with the neon in the window. You hold your breath, watching and shrinking back against the wall. Your hand is again at your throat, trembling.

Dying to Get Out of Here

It is false spring. One of those days when February tries to convince you it's May. And nearly succeeds.

I'm sitting in an examination room in the Digestive Health Center. This austere room has a window with a view of the Sierra Nevada. The sun, even on arctic days, has no trouble finding its way to us. Today it's glaring so strongly off the snow, plunked like a child's ski cap on the top of Mt. Rose, I put on my sunglasses. Here in Reno, we locals joke that there are only three things to do: gamble, get married, and get divorced. I suppose you could put me in the first category, along with everyone else awaiting test results in doctors' offices.

The physician's assistant, dressed in blue scrubs with white sailboats placidly floating over the fabric, has taken my vitals and left me here to wait. I behaved myself, hands folded in my lap, for the first fifteen minutes. But restlessness forces me off the hard table and into whatever trouble I can find. Certificates on the wall tell me the story of an education at the University of Colorado in Denver, and residencies in Internal Medicine and Gastroenterology at the Oregon Health Sciences University completed in 1985. I learn which pedal beside the table causes the back to go up and which brings it back down. When the door opens, I have a purple surgical glove over my mouth and I'm attempting to blow it up like a balloon. If this comes as a surprise to Dr. John Witmer, he gives no indication.

I shrug my shoulders and raise my arms, palms up, in a "What can you do?" gesture, the deflated glove still dangling from my fingers like damning evidence in a court case. I remove my sunglasses and resume my position on the table, hands properly folded again just as he would have found me if only he'd barged in twenty minutes ago.

Dr. Witmer is not a white-coated god of authority. His crisp yellow shirt, striped tie, and impeccable tan trousers give him the appearance of a businessman who was scheduled to attend a luncheon at Montreux Country Club, but somehow wandered in here by mistake. He wraps his foot around the leg of a low-to-the-ground stool and pulls it into the middle of the room. The wheels screech across the tiled floor.

There is a gnawing in me as he rifles through my files, which are multiplying geometrically across the surface of the counter. He rolls back and forth among them more than seems necessary given he must already know most of what's contained there. He was the one who'd punched an eighteen-gauge needle into my chest. His wheels are creaking and scritching.

"I'll get right to the point. I'm afraid the results of your biopsy aren't good," he says. He's pulling on each end of the stethoscope he's tossed around his neck like a boy playing with the string on the hood of his jacket. I say nothing, just raise my eyebrows.

He rubs his thumb and index finger inward across his eyelids until he's left pinching the bridge of his nose. "The condition of your liver indicates you've entered what we call 'third stage.'" He rolls backwards again on those wheels I want to attack with a can of oil. Why am I thinking about wheels and oil when an uncomfortable man is rolling around like a die on a craps table, my life in papers on his lap?

He rolls himself over to a whiteboard on the wall by the door and picks up a black marker. He begins to draw pictures of livers in various stages of disrepair. He creates them without hesitation, like an art student who's been forced to draw sketches of skeletons so many times, he can look straight through flesh without the aid of an X-ray. Superman pops unbidden into my mind. I start to imagine what he would look like walking into a luncheon in blue tights and a red cape with a big red *W* emblazoned on his chest, because, of course, his name is Witmer, so why would he be sporting an *S*? I guess the whole idea is making my lips curl into something resembling a smile, because he puts the cap back on his marker with an irritated click.

"You don't seem to be taking this very seriously. You do understand this isn't good, don't you?" he says.

"Yes, I understand. Go on," I say, hoping my demeanor is suitably sober. His eyebrow is pitched, a caterpillar climbing a precarious branch. What does he want? Tears? Trembling hands? Lips that pucker like they've bitten into a sour mango? Perhaps I didn't study enough to pass the Compliant Patient test. I catch myself starting to apologize, as if I owe him something for his efforts to maintain a professional atmosphere.

He begins again, explaining what Hepatitis C can do to a body, how the virus causes the liver to form tiny scars, scars that act like dams on the Truckee River, impeding its natural movement, starving the river bottom. Liver enzymes, antibodies, viral loads. I feel I've suddenly been seated in a restaurant in Tahiti without the benefit of Berlitz instructional tapes. I keep telling the waiter I want water, and this waiter who doesn't speak English keeps filling my glass with Hinano beer. I swipe the beer foam aside and say, "Can we just get to the bottom line here? How long do I have?"

The consternation that draws over the room shadows his face in a way that even the disingenuous sun, still streaming through the window, would find difficult to lift. Those shadows ask, "Don't you realize that he's rehearsed an entire dramatic monologue, complete with scenery and props? Why are you stopping him before he's reached the second act?" I'm too eager for the denouement.

"Okay, bottom line. You have roughly five to eight years left. Eventually you'll develop jaundice, maybe even liver cancer. Your kidneys will shut down in concert with your liver. Then comes coma. Then death," he chokes out.

"Is it a painful death?" I ask.

Both of us are distracted then by murmurs slipping through the thin walls that separate us from the rest. Other doctors and other patients in similar rooms, each playing their own games of roulette. Odds, safe bets, risks. Outcomes.

"Sometimes it is," he says. "However, I've had alcoholic patients with livers so damaged, I wonder how they can drag themselves into my office. But they manage without many complaints. They keep going to the same bar every night and one morning, they don't wake up with a hangover or even a heartbeat. The progression of cirrhosis is a very individual process."

His wheels protest as he rolls over to shine his penlight in my eyes. He's looking for something beyond disease. Finally a *hmmm* slips from his lips and into my ear. There it is. He's excavated it. Denial. Even first-year residents know the stages of grief.

What he can't see behind those retinas is the husband who had died three years prior in our bed while I was sleeping right next to him. There are no visible bruises from my failed attempts at CPR. No abrasions to show the trampling down the hallway of emergency personnel dressed in firemen's garb and weighty boots with metal clasps. Life-sustaining equipment, too many hands beating on a naked body that had been dragged from the bed, been laid on the floor, and was already gone, though they attempted valiantly for over an hour to change that fact. No sighting of the rescue helicopter in the backyard, whipping the sagebrush with its wings, waiting to scoop him up in its claws, and drag him away to an ER where they would continue to flail on his chest with their fists and puncture him with their needles. We never got that far. A female EMT delivered the news that he was beyond what the helicopter could hope to prevent. They sent the black bird away with empty talons.

She walked me into the bedroom and respectfully shut the door as she left. There was blood and feces spread across the carpet in abstract Kandinsky patterns. I knelt beside my husband in the middle of it. They'd thrown a white sheet over him and it was tucked up under his chin. He smelled of vomit, and though they'd made some elementary efforts to make him presentable, there were pieces of the roast beef he'd eaten the night before still clinging to his hair.

I'd never been alone with a dead body. What is expected of you in a circumstance like this? I was a teacher who'd been in many classrooms, but no classroom I'd ever entered conducted these kinds of lessons. What do you do over the body of the person you've worked, eaten, bathed, and slept with since you were twenty-four years old? What final words do you say to the man who has formed you, in some benevolent Pygmalion fashion, not into whatever his vision dictates you should be, but rather into what you would have created yourself if only you'd had the vision to know how far your own potential would allow you to evolve?

I threw the sheet aside and ran my palms over the entire length of him. Not in some futile attempt to memorize his muscular structure, nor in a laying on of hands. My fingers acted only as fingers will when they want to crawl inside something. I put my lips to his lips. I held his limp penis. I finally understood a necrophiliac's predilections. This was the penis, he'd joked, that would allow me to identify him on a slab in the morgue even if he'd been decapitated. It was mottled by vitiligo, parts of it lighter, parts of it darker, just as Mt. Rose looked today with the sunlight and the shadows chasing each other over its contours. It was a penis unlike any of the billions of penises that have walked the planet. I haven't any idea how long I might have stayed in that position, if there hadn't been a courteous knock on the door. I covered him again and hung my head, guilty of abuse.

I lift my face. Dr. Witmer's assistant is poking her head into the room to tell him he has an urgent telephone call. He sighs, and closes my folder. He apologizes and says he must take it. I'm left alone again with only my thoughts to occupy me. The purple surgical glove is out of reach.

Two brawny EMTs had arrived to adjust my husband's body on their gurney. They rolled it down the hallway with me beside it, positions we'd assumed many times when he was a patient being taken into surgery. The wheels of the gurney screeched against their own metal legs. There were no embraces, no "I'll see you in the recovery room." Only me, my head on his silent chest, speaking as if he could still hear. Wild words about the monster that is diabetes, my belief in stem cell research, my assurances to continue to fight for a cure. Promises choking on my own spit. A disjointed impromptu eulogy.

When we reached the front door, one of the EMTs respectfully uncurled my hand from the side of the gurney. He was crying. He flattened my palm, and placed something onto its creviced surface. Something that settled against the heart line. It was my husband's wedding ring. The same ring I am now twirling in circles on my thumb while listening to this doctor who's returned to my room, and is now proceeding without me onto the subject of treatment options.

"You have a genotype of the virus that is not responsive to treatment in a majority of cases," he says. "We currently use a treatment protocol that includes two drugs, interferon and ribaviron."

He fills my extended hands with a packet of papers. I blink my eyes to better focus on an encyclopedia's worth of side effects. The list begins with the merely annoying like headaches and fevers, and progresses to the truly magnificent like blindness and deafness, the last of which must have struck me prematurely. Words are continuing to flow past me, undammed by any scars. I finally hear him clearly when he concludes with, "So, stop by the appointment desk and they'll schedule you for the first shot."

"Let me get this straight," I say. "You want to inject me with drugs over the course of the next year that have at best a 33 percent chance of working, that cost $5,000 a month not covered by insurance I don't have, and that could leave me deaf and blind, but still uncured?"

I'm not sure whether it's him or his wheels that cough. "I told you the news wasn't good. You owe it to yourself to give this treatment regimen a chance. I can't promise you much, but I can promise you that if you don't, you *will* die prematurely."

Though I don't have his penlight, I do look into his eyes, which have some measure of softness to them behind the stern recommendations and grave warnings. But there is not a trace there of a ride on the back of a rented motorcycle fifteen years ago, my arms around the waist of a man who was trying his best to pilot a vehicle with a broken headlight through the encroaching darkness that was embracing the peak of Mt. Otemanu on Bora Bora, and sliding down its torso. No indication of the kind of trust that can overshadow any thought of what might happen should the front tire hit a rut. Only the terrifying beauty of stars spread across the sky like atoms in a crystalline structure, in a place that has no pollution, streetlights, or clouds to hamper anyone's vision. A sunset such a vivid shade of violet, the first thing you do when you return home is order yourself a pair of contact lenses in that shade and wear that impossible color every day. So that whenever that man might want to return to the dirt road that was hardly a road circling the most leeward island, all he need do is look in your eyes.

I was forty-four years old when my husband died. Sitting on this table, I imagine I face approximately forty more years in solitary confinement. This doctor is telling me I can commute that prison sentence by three-quarters simply by doing nothing. He's handing me a free ticket back to my seat behind a man laughing on a broken motorcycle, riding like two children who didn't have the sense God gave to the dogs smart enough to lie in patches of island grasses and merely watch.

"There won't be any need for another appointment," I say as I reach for my sunglasses and prepare to hop off the table. "Thank you. I'll take the free ticket. We're done, right?"

"Free ticket?" he asks. He shakes his head. "There are no free tickets. You're just going to walk out of here? You don't want to discuss this any further?" He rolls his stool close enough to put a hand on my knee. "I can't in good conscience let you do that without trying to change your mind. I don't think you understand the serious implications of all this. The longer you go without treatment, the smaller the window gets. Eventually it will slam shut. Then no treatment will stand a chance of helping you." The big red *W* on his chest is growing smaller with each passing minute.

"I understand plenty," I say.

"You might as well go home, sit down at your desk, and write a suicide note," he says as he pushes off from my knee and wheels himself under the window, back where his stool had started. His suddenly curt tone is probably his last-ditch effort to shock patients into seeing the light. But I'd already seen the lights. No ride on his scritchy-wheeled stool could compete.

I climb off the table and stand beside him, my hand on his shoulder.

"It's okay. Really," I say.

He swallows roughly. There is a knot that pushes against his Adam's apple, making it more prominent. A story of his own carried behind the larynx, beyond the reach of diagnostic tools, outside the influence of medicine.

I pluck my jacket from the hook and slide my arms through the sleeves. I tuck my sunglasses in my pocket. He follows me down the hallway in silence. My papers land with a thud on his assistant's desk, and he prepares to enter a different, but identical exam room. He reaches to grab the patient folder that's been left for him in a rack on the door. The file slips, and reports fall in a shower of white petals that drop at his feet. He leans his forehead against the wall for a moment before bending to gather them up.

I push through the door and into false spring. Did you know the sun has a smell? It's remarkably like Tiare Tahiti. I will go home and immediately follow doctor's orders. I will sit down at my desk and write this. It isn't a suicide note. It's a love letter.

Susan Dobrof

This Morning

I wake to one breath's worth of peace. Then fire flares in my leg, sets kneecap throbbing, lobbing spears into calf and shin. The burn sears the arch of my foot, igniting heel and toes. I flip the bedside light on and rip the comforter off the leg, expecting to see swollen flesh, bright red from thigh to aching toes. But no. Pale skin, dry skin, conceals the feverish spasm.

The clock glares 6:03 a.m., too early for this body to wake. Two tabs of Neurontin and one of Trazodone the night before used to buy enough sleep, but not now. Not here, in an "exacerbation"—multiple sclerosis jargon for *worsening*. I shake a Xanax from its plastic bottle onto my tongue and roll it around my mouth. Tasting enough chalky grains to calm, but not stupefy, I spit the pill onto the nightstand. The blaze snakes up, pushes into my thigh. My mind launches Buddhist prayers.

> *May I be happy, may all beings be happy.*
>
> *May I be healthy, may this body be well. May all beings be healthy.*
>
> *May I be free from inner and outer harm, may all beings be free from inner and outer harm.*
>
> *May I know ease and joy. May all beings know ease and joy.*

Drugs and prayers, prayers and drugs. Still I do not sleep or grow calm.

I remember the self that could swim, muscular legs propelling strong body from one end of the pool to the other. At the beach, those former feet strode across cool, damp sand onto the warmer stuff that coats toes and heels. They outran the Frisbee sailing overhead, stop, twist and one deft hand snatched the disc behind my back.

The pit of my stomach churns, sends waves of sorrow through my chest and into my throat and eyes. Tears, mucus, drip, and mix. Swinging legs from bed to floor, I see withered calf muscles above feet too weak to walk in sand. The paved promenade at Seaside on my scooter, legs encased in braces and shoes, is as close to the beach as I get now.

My rib cage shudders, then settles. I ground these feet on the wood floor, take a deep breath, and trudge out of the fire into the cool day. *May I know ease and joy.*

Anne Gudger

Black Sharpie

"You'll want to write his name in his clothes," says a fifty-something nurse here at St. Francis Hospital in Federal Way, her hand dusting my forearm. "Everything," she adds. "You'd be shocked by what gets lost at a nursing home."

My stomach buckles and somersaults. I can't. Write in his clothes? My stepdad would be pissed.

"Really," she insists nodding her head, her wavy gray hair waving. "I'll get you a Sharpie." She disappears to the nurses' station full of blinking lights, impatient phones, and permanent markers.

Deface J.'s clothes? No. But I have to. Mom with her head in her hands, shoulders slumped, full of *I'm not built for battle*. I'm elected Marker of the Clothes. I breathe deep to imagine a different scenario: packing for summer camp just like I used to do for my kids. I cradle J.'s clothes—a pile of pants and shirts and T-shirts and slip-on shoes. I pop the cap off the Sharpie. That permanent marker smell hits me, punctuating what I have to do.

❖ ❖ ❖

J. is my stepdad. Some say stepfather but he's so much more. English doesn't have enough labels for family relationships. He's my other dad. My second dad. The hero dad who rode in when I was ten. Not the weekend Dad I also loved; J. was the daily dad who loved us three girls—Lisa 13, me 10, and Janis 5—like we were his from the start. He drove us to ice skating, to the ski bus before sunrise; he taught me how to fish for trout, swallow a pill, wash a car down to shining the whitewalls, change the oil in my car. He stressed the importance of not wearing too much perfume ("We don't want to smell you before we see you") and eating healthy ("Have some. It'll grow hair on your chest").

When he and Mom came home from their honeymoon more than forty years ago, I hurled myself against his chest, squealing, "Can I call you Dad now?"

He smiled and said, "Sure, Kid. If you want. That'd be nice. But I don't want to offend your dad." He rubbed the top of my head with his knuckles.

"I have two dads," I said and squeezed his waist. "I'm lucky that way."

I've said it all these years: two dads. Lucky me. Two granddads for my kids. Lucky them.

❖ ❖ ❖

Bright overhead lights and disinfectant bring me back to my marking chore. *Summer camp,* I tell myself. *Imagine he's going to camp.* I plunk on the hard hospital hall floor, legs folded beneath me. A lanky young man pushes the lunch cart packed with pressed turkey and gray gravy down the hall, the wheels squeaking on the polished speckled linoleum.

I smooth each piece of clothing and write "J. Upton" in tidy block letters. Robin's egg blue polo. Khaki pants. Tube socks. White boxers. Merrell slip-ons. "Even his hat?" I ask the nurse as she bristles by me and my graffiti project. "Hat, too." I rub my hand across the crown of his hat—one of many in a series of Irish wool walking hats with their short brims and distinctive M-shaped profiles. I bought him one when I was studying in England my junior year of college and he's worn this style ever since, almost thirty years.

The bridge of my nose pinches like it does before I cry. My throat gets thick and straw-sized.

Summer camp, summer camp, summer camp, I repeat, mantra-like. I take a big breath, mutter "shit" and start.

On the inside of the brim, the sweatband, I print "J. Upton" all in caps. J. Just like that because it's really his name. Just one letter.

Will he need bug spray? Tent poles? Playing cards? I think about the times I've readied my kids for camps: Scout camp, Outdoor School, Snowboard camp.

"Do you have to write my name in my undies?" First Jake (the oldest) then Maria (the youngest) protested.

"Yeah, I do. But I'll leave our phone number off, okay?"

"Mo-om," both kids took their turn saying. Jake with his palms raised. Maria with her fists on her hips.

I try to imagine my stepdad paddling a canoe, grumbling at craft time, over-

---

She Holds the Face of the World

toasting his marshmallows. Zinc oxide on his nose. Mosquito bites dotting his arms and legs like constellations. But I can't. Camp is too far from the nursing home.

J. had a stroke. He's spent five days in the hospital, climbing in and out of consciousness, deciding if he is staying in his body, or if it's time to die. My mom and sisters and I have been here, sitting and sleeping in his hospital room, wondering what he'll do, wondering how we'll live if this anchor of a man pulls up anchor.

❖   ❖   ❖

The morning of J.'s stroke, my older sister Lisa called: "J.'s weak. Mom and I are trying to get him to sit up and eat breakfast. He's a wet noodle. What should we do?"

I was home, 150 miles away in Portland. "Call 911," I told her. "I'll pack a bag and be there in three hours."

Fast packing. Fast driving. The whole time thinking about this huge change in J. He is in the early stages of dementia, but still himself in many ways—quick with a joke, a smile. He's slow, but he feeds and dresses himself. He gets annoyed if we do things for him where he's capable. What happened that he couldn't sit up?

I got to the emergency room in time to hear a doctor ask, "Who's the president?"

"A friend of mine," my stepdad said.

I had just slipped in his curtained room, quiet. Not wanting to be here. Not wanting to not be here.

"Okay, but can you tell me his name?" the ER doctor pushed, his oversized hand cupping J.'s shoulder.

J. stared at me. I almost mouthed "Obama."

"Mr. Upton?"

J. shrugged, pushed out his lower lip. "We had to get rid of George's son," he said.

Later, upstairs in a hospital bed, he guessed at the year ("1998? '99?"). Before dementia he'd managed an auto parts warehouse for twenty-five years where he rattled off part numbers and knew how many filters were in stock. He was a detail guy who built his own stereo from a Heathkit and subscribed to a pile of electronic and woodworking magazines. J. fabricated his own woodworking jigs when Home Depot didn't have what he needed.

Now he couldn't touch the end of his nose with his fingertip. He thought he was at a military base. He told a doctor he was talking to God.

"What's God saying, Mr. Upton?" the internist asked, dark hair, dark eyes, dark skin. From Pakistan I thought, that lyrical lilt in her voice. My mom, sisters, and I leaned in.

"He's talking about home," J. said with a sigh. "It might be time to come home."

That night my sisters and I kept vigil: changing guard between the hard vinyl loveseat down the hall and dozing in J.'s room in the visitors' recliner chair that doesn't really recline. J. tossed his covers off, clutched at his hospital gown, kicked his legs and swung his arms. All night long he cycled between resting and flailing.

In the morning a curly-headed nurse with bubble gum pink lipstick asked him, "Mr. Upton, do you know where you are?"

He studied the ceiling.

"Mr. Upton? Do you know where you are?"

J. stared at the holes in the acoustical tiles.

"Yeah. A hole in the universe," he said.

She thought for a beat. Scratched her forearm. "Do you know why you're here?"

"I fell through."

A hole in the universe. A narrow passageway. A sliver of a life that was big with racing motorcycles, woodworking, gardening, fox-trotting, fixing anything that needed fixing in the house; a life that was big with Mom and us girls; a life full of music and books and philosophical talks; a life peppered with smoking a pipe, sipping Jack Daniels and always choosing Chinese food for take-out. That big life shrunk to Cheerios for breakfast, a morning nap, the History Channel on TV, another nap, lunch and dinner and more sleeping. That hole in the universe travels one way. It doesn't have room for all his loves.

❖ ❖ ❖

I slip J.'s folded, marked clothes into a plastic hospital bag: St. Francis Hospital printed on the side. After medical transport arrives, I hound the staff until discharge papers are signed. Two drivers load J. up to drive him less than one mile to Garden Terrace—a nursing home my sisters and I picked because the staff to patient ratio is high, it's clean and doesn't smell like urine.

Mom, J., Lisa, Janis and I arrive at Garden Terrace with its soft yellow exterior and dusty rose interior. We're nomads who lost their one bag. Mom and Lisa are going to stay the first night in J.'s room so Lisa and I make a flying, buying trip through Fred Meyer's. In a crazed rush we buy a sleeping bag, sweats for Mom, a TV with a built-in DVD, *ET* and *Moonstruck*, bananas and Chips Ahoy cookies. All set for the night. Mom and Lisa hunker down with J., worry about him, worry about his care, worry about the future.

The dad who arrives at Garden Terrace is still, as my sister said, a wet noodle. He can't walk, sit up, support himself. He can talk—slowly, with long pauses around his end of the conversation. He can feed himself. Sort of. His trembling hand moves the spoon close, just short of his mouth. I watch him eat with my mouth open, willing him to ape the gap. I want to hold his spoon, like I did when my kids were small. I want to play airplane, make the spoon dip and dive: "Here comes the plane. Open the hanger. Here it comes. Vrrrrmm."

We've changed places. We hear this all the time that the child becomes the parent. When I ask my mom to close a door, we both laugh. When my mom asks me if I've seen her keys, we laugh. The lighter side of role reversal. But I look at J. and I don't feel like laughing. I ache for him. The man in front of me is a shrunken edition of the strong dad who was six feet tall. 200 pounds. A man who could move furniture on his own and still pick me up when I hit my adult size. Now he's 170 pounds and can barely lift a spoon.

❖ ❖ ❖

The next four months are punctured with small strokes and more steps down the one-way dementia road. Hospital. Nursing home. Hospital. Nursing home. If I drew J.'s moves it would be one heavy line scribbled back and forth. What next? J. needed more care than Mom could provide. Their home of thirty-seven years got struck off the options list. Best choice: assisted living.

We move them from their home of thirty-seven years with the view of Puget Sound (deep blue water, cloudy skies, clear skies, tug boats, sail boats, power boats, smells of salt water, and worn rocks) and cupboards full of memories and J.'s workshop packed with tools and projects he loved. We move them to a one-bedroom assisted-living apartment at Foundation House. We pack favorite things—two stuffed bookcases, family pictures spanning great grandparents to grandkids, blown-glass vases, Limoges china for four, an antique mantle clock, an antique mantle queen, motorcycles trophies, swimming trophies, a portrait of Mom my daughter drew when she was five. Their bulletin board that used to be a collage of Christmas card pictures, art from my kids and love notes ("Cobbler's in the fridge. Enjoy! Love the Cobbler Fairy") is now covered in shopping lists for the drug store, doctor appointment reminder cards and emergency phone numbers. My sisters' and my cell phone numbers are tacked up there twice.

While my parents are together, it is not the life they imagined.

I want to do the impossible: Right J. and Mom's world.

When my kids were small it was easy to soothe them, wipe their tears, hold them, come up with silly stuff that made them feel better, assure them everything would be okay.

I want to do the same for J.—pick him up, wipe him off. But he's much too big. And unlike my kids, he won't be growing into his shoes and getting ready for kindergarten. He's at the other end of life. And I know how this part of the adventure ends.

He's shutting down. He spends a lot of time turned inward. The man who loved the five-foot-big-head-only portraits I drew of him and Mom in the sand at the beach with a stick as large as my ten-year-old self, who cheered and put me on his shoulders so I could take pictures of my beach drawings, is quiet now, withdrawn. No more getting excited over teaching little Janis to ride a bike, or saying, "Hold tight and lean with me" as we girls took turns on the back of his motorcycle. No more explaining how an engine works (car, motorcycle, lawnmower) while daughters and a generation later grandkids plopped on a tall yellow stool in his workshop and smelled his pipe—his own blend of cherry tobacco and Sir Walter Raleigh. That man is gone, gone, gone.

The older he gets, the younger he becomes. He lets my family and me feed him, cut his fingernails, wipe up spilled food and drink. When I put his hat on his nearly bald head, his glasses on his face, his napkin under his chin, he doesn't protest. He smiles. The sweetest smile. Angelic. Wrinkles fan out around his blue eyes—the shade of blue that's somewhere between sky blue and sea blue and I can't help but think that's where my dad is now: between the sky and the sea.

❖ ❖ ❖

Tick off another four months. One. Two. Three. Four.

When I visited my parents at their apartment last week, J. was having a good day: awake and talking. I got there just after lunch. Mom and J. are still adjusting to communal dining—dining room packed with seniors, walkers parked along the walls, wheelchairs scooted up to the tables, a sign next to the coffee pot: "We'll serve you. Please don't serve yourself"—after so many years of mostly eating with just each other and the calm of Puget Sound.

"Any good lunch stories?" I asked.

"Oh, there's always something," Mom said and sighed as she hung J.'s tweed hat with "J. Upton" printed inside on the coat rack. "Gert didn't want to let this man sit with her. She thought he was her old neighbor who was mean to her dog."

J. rubbed his chin with his thumb and forefinger. "Wherever there are people, there are fruitcakes," he said.

"Oh, J.," Mom said, her frown wrinkles deepening.

He raised his hands, palms skyward. "What?"

"Nothing." Mom shrugged.

J. slumped in his wingback chair, glad to be out of his wheelchair. He wanted out of his slippers and into his shoes.

"You okay?" I asked as he struggled with his slippers.

"Yeah, are you?"

He scuffed the heel of each slipper against the carpet a few times, finally flipping them off. He tried to slip on his slip-ons—the same shoes I'd written "J. Upton" in eight months ago when I sat on the hospital floor and made myself be strong; when I thought, *You never really grow up until you write your parent's name in his clothes.*

The backs of his shoes squished down, like how I'd smash my shoes when I was a kid to turn sneakers into clogs. He leaned over to pull up the backs, but couldn't lean far enough without losing his balance. I instinctively put my arm out in front of him, like I have for years if I'm driving and brake suddenly with a kid in the front seat.

"Hey, Dad, can I help you with those?" I asked and pointed to his shoes.

"Sure, Kid. Why not," he said and smiled.

I smiled too because he hadn't called me "Kid" in a long time.

"I sure like these shoes," I said as I slipped off the couch and crouched in front of him. I picked up his suede shoes and held them in my lap, rubbed the tops with my thumbs.

"They're so soft." I pulled back the instep to widen the opening for his size 11 feet. He inched his feet in as I pulled up the backs in the same way I used to slide my children's little feet into their shoes. One at a time. Left. Right.

"They're a little big for you, Kid," he said. "But some day you can have them."

❖ ❖ ❖

Two years later and deeper dementia and more small strokes and then pneumonia (hospice's angel some call it) and J. dies, pulls up anchor. We're brokenhearted and sad and relieved and aching and missing him all wadded up. Such a big life come to an end. Such a beautiful man. Such a generous heart. We give away those nice suede shoes. Too big for me and Mom and my sisters and husband and kids. But not his hats. I have one and so do my sisters and my mom and my daughter and my aunt. Irish wool walking hats like the one I bought him thirty years ago. Narrow brim; an M profile. Years of my stepdad in his hats. Mine has "J. Upton" carefully printed in my block letters on the sweatband.

I wear it every cool day, especially in the rain.

Cara Holman

30 Degrees from the Horizon

It is cold. I am cold. Very, very cold. I startle at the sound of my brother's voice on the other end of the line. I have forgotten I was talking with him. "What do you see?" he is asking. I look up at the sky. "I see the roof," I say. There is a slight pause. "Of course," he says. "It's too low in the sky to view from the deck. You'll have to go down to the orchard." I nod, until I remember he can't see me. "Yes," I say. "Better take a flashlight," he adds, "and watch for gopher holes."

I go back to the house and grab a flashlight from the table in the entry. On second thought, I also slip on a pair of gloves that are lying there. They are too big for me, and my fingers wiggle around loosely inside the finger holes, making it difficult to keep my grip on the phone. Down in the orchard, he describes where to look. I feel like a detective. It is thirty degrees from the horizon, towards the west. I know west. It is away from the bay, towards the shadowy shape of the foothills. My brother knows his stars. He is an astronomer.

"What do you see now?" he asks. I look. I see lots of stars. "Lots of stars," I say. I am standing in the middle of their orchard at night, looking at stars. What was their orchard, I silently amend. Was. Is. I am beginning to sort out verb tenses now. It is almost making sense. They lived here once. They lived. "It's the brightest one," he says. "You can't miss it." I look some more. Some stars are faint, some are bright. I compare them all in my mind. "I think I see it now," I finally say, my voice rising above the wind. For a moment I stand in silence, thinking of him 2,000 miles away, viewing the same star, from a different angle.

>   deep cold—
>   looking for
>   a lost star

Alida Thacher

The Bösendorfer

It takes five years to create each Bösendorfer Grand Piano. It takes a lifetime to hear all that yours has come to tell you.

The beauty of my Bösendorfer overwhelmed me: cased in walnut with inlaid gold; massive elegantly shaped legs, brass pedals, a hand-carved music rack. It was strung with lower tensile wire, and its bass strings were made of iron, as they were in the nineteenth century. The ivory keys were yellowed with a century of musicians' fingertips. The delicacy of its details was a counterpoint to its immensity. Seven feet long and five feet wide, it sprawled grandly across my living room floor like a small airplane.

When Franz Liszt gave concerts, he would pound into the notes so forcefully that it was not uncommon for him to break the strings of three or four pianos each night. Several extra instruments were kept off-stage as replacements. Finally they built him a Bösendorfer.

The exquisite simple beauty of the overtones in a single note can move the soul to tears.

And recognizing that I have to get rid of mine also moves my soul to tears.

My great uncle Samuel gave it to me. He was a concert pianist, the toast of Europe during the teens and twenties. From Boston, he studied at the New England Conservatory of Music, mentored by Arnold Schönberg and Eric Satie. He never married. The Archduchess Gisela of Austria presented him with his Bösendorfer after attending a series of Beethoven sonatas that she believed were responsible for the birth of her long prayed-for son.

My mother was his favored niece. She was also a musical prodigy, mastering the cello by the age of six to play "Claire de Lune" to a spellbound group of judges at the Röthenberg Festival. They awarded her the Plume D'Or, despite the fierce competition from ten adults who had over 150 years of concert performance experience between them.

It is love that makes me do it, of course: love and devotion and commitment.

Buoyed by their success at Mother's Plume D'Or, my great uncle and grandparents ratcheted up her career path. She was sent to a private school half-days; the other half of her days were spent practicing her cello, being coached in theater and choreography, and performing. Uncle Samuel frequently flew in from Budapest or Tokyo or Cairo to practice with her. She was forced to wear long ringlets and short skirts and anklets with little white flats well past sixth grade. In other words, she began that age-old anti-feminist tradition of lying about her age sometime around her seventh year. The theory was that she would compete much better the younger she appeared. She was an outcast with her peers, treated like a freak, laughed at and teased. But it wasn't until she was twelve, when she shot up to 5 feet 6 inches, and the extreme self-consciousness of puberty began to smother her like a blanket, that she started to deeply resent her family.

The Bösendorfer factory owns a forest outside of Vienna. It is the job of one man to go out and knock on trees to hear which one should become the next piano. When the right one is chosen, it is felled, and then it cures outside for several years. Living through the seasons, the rains and harsh sunshine and winds and snows, it becomes wise enough to be a Bösendorfer.

In her first year of high school, my mother snapped. She refused to touch her instrument, insisted on public school, and lived out four very rebellious years. Then she went on to college, majored in accounting, and married my father, who was working on his MBA. Uncle Samuel threatened to disown her, but then I arrived.

When I was born, Uncle Samuel gave us a baby grand for a christening gift. By this time, my mother had become rather sentimental about music education (although not her own), and she saw that our household was filled with classical recordings during waking and sleeping hours. I loved it. My first word was *forte*; my earliest memory was throwing up at Handel's *Messiah*.

After the wood for the Bösendorfer has seasoned, each Bösendorfer is hand-crafted, a process that takes sixty-eight weeks. It's said that each instrument picks up personality traits and emotions of those who work on her. If a technician is angry—if his wife has left him or he has quarreled with a friend—the action on the piano he works on will be too hard. If he is sad or insecure, she will hit too soft.

My mother began to formally teach me piano at the age of two and a half. She would lift me onto the piano seat, cover my hands with her hands, and guide me through scales and chords, simple melodies and bass lines. By the time I was four, I was sight-reading, and by the time I was six, I could play all of Chopin's mazurkas with my eyes closed. At nine, I got my first invitation to solo with the symphony.

At my mother's insistence I went to public school every day, but I spent the time between school and dinner at the conservatory as part of the young musicians program, studying under every maestro. I usually spent an hour on homework each evening, but after that, I practiced several hours more before my father sent me off to bed. Uncle Samuel would arrange performances for me several times a year, usually scheduled during school vacations. He would meet me in some faraway city like Amsterdam or San Francisco, and we together would dazzle our audiences with Beethoven and Rachmaninoff and Bach.

The sanders working on the Bösendorfer hang pictures of naked women on the walls of their work area. They claim this is so that when they work the piano, she will feel like the flesh of a woman's body.

This was my life through high school, and then upon graduation I entered the conservatory full-time, where I remain today. Great Uncle Samuel was delighted with my passion for the piano and supported me entirely. He began by funding my lessons, then the tuition for the young musicians program, and then he paid for all living and schooling expenses when I became a full-time conservatory student. He rarely missed a recital or concert of mine.

I think he never got over his heartbreak from my mother's rejection of the cello, and never quite trusted her influence over me, so when I turned twenty-one, and he was well into his eighties, he flew into town to find me respectable living quarters. Time to cut the apron strings, he told me. He worried that if he wasn't there to help me, I might never leave my parents' home. He took me from one flat to the next around town, clearly driven by some kind of inner vision, and when he found it, he knew immediately. It was a sunny two bedroom on the second floor. It had an enormous living room, with a wide balcony overlooking the park. It was acoustically perfect. The walls, ceiling and floor were soundproof; there was never any indication that anyone else lived in the building except for occasional sightings at the mailboxes. Don't worry about furniture, he told me. I'll take care of that.

So in a couple of weeks after the sale closed, furniture trucks arrived with a long couch and a couple of leather armchairs and a velvet chaise longue, a bureau, and a queen-sized bed. In another delivery truck came elaborate kitchen furnishings and boxes and boxes of musical scores.

But the biggest surprise came in the final truck. It became abundantly clear why Uncle Samuel was only satisfied by a place with a living room the size of a ballroom and wide double doors to the balcony. He had sent his beloved Bösendorfer, along with a crew of men who had to remove the outside doors and hoist the massive piano up over the balcony and through the entry.

The Bösendorfer is known for her warm clear sound, as well as her power, both fluid and suggestive. Those who own a Bösendorfer swear she is alive, that she understands those who play it, for better or worse. She speaks, and she listens to you. She understands your feelings, and reflects them back to you like a mirror of acoustics. She forms with her musician an unbreakable bond.

Uncle Samuel died shortly after my Bösendorfer arrived, able to let go knowing it was both safe and adored.

My life was very sweet those days. I had begun teaching and was happy giving lessons, taking classes and playing recitals. I couldn't learn enough about music history and theory. I felt content to spend the rest of my life at the conservatory, and thanks to Uncle Samuel's stipend, I could afford it.

My days consisted of rising around eight, eating a bowl of oatmeal, practicing on the Bösendorfer for an hour, then catching the 9:40 bus to school. I took classes and gave lessons until 5:30, then took the 5:45 back to my flat. On weekends, when I wasn't performing, I would spend most hours practicing, except for Sunday night dinners at my parents.

I met Sarah a few months after I began teaching, a complete surprise to me, although she told me later she had been planning it. She took the 9:40 bus to her job at the mall—she sold shoes—and since she got on at an earlier stop and got off after I did, she was able to observe me through my entire ride. I was oblivious, as I was about most of what went on around me. One day, as I was studying Ravel's *Gaspard de la Nuit*, an exceedingly complicated score, she sat in the empty seat next to me and offered me some peanuts. I looked up, startled, and found myself staring into her large sea-green eyes, at her plump pink lips and her thick smooth black hair that reached down her back. Her beauty shocked me.

She began asking me about the music I was reading and what the conservatory was like and what instrument I played. I am generally very quiet, but I found it easy to talk to her from the moment I met her. She started saving a seat for me, and after about a week, she held my hand as we rode. (I would have been much too shy to take her hand first!) We began to meet for coffee. At the end of the day, she came to the conservatory, and we walked to the local café frequented by music students. There she told me the story of her life.

When she was a baby, her father died in the war—the silly one, she said, although she thought all wars were silly. Her mother never formed another long attachment, and Sarah remained an only child. They moved frequently, her mother dabbling in climates: the steamy languor of Louisiana; the deep snows, lush summers, and brilliant autumns of northern Michigan; the soggy winters of the Pacific Northwest; the dry sunny heat of the Nevada desert.

They had moved here two years ago, just in time for Sarah's high school graduation. At that point, she decided to jump off the moving train of her mother's momentum, answered a "roommate-wanted" ad, and relocated into a wild household of four men and two women who never seemed to sleep or clean. She did have her own room, a tiny thing between the living room and the only bathroom.

She had held a series of jobs since then: a receptionist for a law firm (she couldn't afford the clothes); a waitress at a German restaurant (she experienced paralyzing stage fright when required to sing "Happy Birthday" with the accordionist); an oil jockey with Jiffy Lube (she couldn't do it in under ten minutes). She had been selling shoes at Florsheim's for the last six months, and she liked the quiet carpeted floors and the soft padding of stockinged feet.

Every day I was more entranced. I had problems concentrating on my work. My mind wandered, imagining whom Sarah was fitting for shoes or thinking about the cobalt blue sweater she wore the day before. I was falling in love quickly and didn't quite know what to do. I invited her to my flat for dinner. We decided on Saturday, since neither of us had to work the next day. I was nervous, of course, and spent the day cleaning and making eggplant Parmesan and playing romantic sonatas on the Bösendorfer.

When she arrived, a little late, she was visibly overwhelmed by my flat. I was overwhelmed by her scent, her formfitting red dress, and her hair swept atop her head, exposing that long graceful neck. Of course she would notice my Bösendorfer first. She had never seen a grand piano except on television, certainly never the enormous Bösendorfer. She asked me to play something for her. I was glad, since I was almost faint from nerves and emotion, and the Bösendorfer was the only thing that could focus me.

I warmed up with a Bach fugue, then moved on to a lovely Chopin waltz. Next, I began Beethoven's *Opus 110*, but I was only in the second movement when she put her arms around my neck and whispered in my ear, asking if I knew any Celine Dion. She had met her in line at the Las Vegas Safeway and said she was the nicest person in the world.

When I told her unhappily that Celine Dion was not in my repertoire, she kissed me deeply, and pulled me into the bedroom.

I had never been with a woman before, but I had a lifetime of experience exploring the tones, power, and sensuality of a finely tuned instrument. Her skin was like smooth mahogany, and her responses to my caresses were immediate but varied, depending on how hard or soft I stroked her, whether I caressed her navel or bottom. When I took her breast in my mouth, I suddenly understood why men played the trumpet. Although I would have been content to explore the nooks and crannies of her body for hours, she wanted *poco più allegro*. She guided my head between her legs, and I played her like a piccolo, *staccato non troppo*. Her body arpeggioed. Then I penetrated her, *forte*, then *pianissimo*, then *forte, forte, forte, crescendo, fortissimo!* And our arpeggios shook the bed and our voices sang out and I thanked Uncle Samuel for the flat's great acoustics.

That night I got up, naked, and pounded out some Beethoven, then Shostakovich, then Tchaikovsky. The Bösendorfer sparkled with my joy. I was tired and somewhat sore and had never felt so alive in my life.

We made love again in the early morning, *pianissimo, dolce*. I kissed her eyelashes and her forehead and her ears and drifted off to sleep.

I couldn't get enough of Sarah, her smell like lavender and ylang ylang, her taste like popcorn and marshmallows. I loved her voice. She spoke in a melodic drawl, low and sexy like an oboe snaking through the grass, and her laughter chimed like a carillon. Every time I caught sight of her—buttoning her blouse, opening the refrigerator, brushing her teeth—the intensity of my desire almost hurt.

She moved in soon after. We were spending every night together anyway. She brought over a few possessions: an Indian bedspread, a Crock-Pot, a small television set. Her dresses fit easily in my closet—I'd never been much on clothes.

I stopped playing the Bösendorfer in the evenings, since the noise bothered her, and besides, she told me, she was jealous of my time. Instead we huddled under the blankets and watched *American Idol* and *Nanny 911*. When I woke early, I would quietly close the door and tiptoe to the piano, playing soft chords and scales and bass lines. But if Sarah woke, I would feel her stare from the doorway, arms crossed, before she would urge me back to bed.

After a while, Sarah stopped going to work. When I worried about it, she told me not to, that it was a lousy job. Every evening it seemed I came home from the conservatory to surprises—her black underwear strewn across the dining room table, a jar of Cheez Whiz open on the counter, chairs pushed oddly around the living room floor.

She frequently begged me to stay home with her, and for the first time in my life, I began to skip my lessons. We would spend much of the day making love, then we would walk through the park or shop for groceries or stroll through neighborhoods looking at houses we would someday buy. She didn't let me near the piano—those days, she said, were all hers; she wasn't sharing.

I began to miss my Bösendorfer exceedingly, to crave her. When I walked through the door, I would run my hand across her sleek shiny top. I would sit on the piano bench to talk to Sarah about her day, although she would soon take my hands and pull me to the couch. I found I could never play my piano, since Sarah was always home when I was, and it was clear she wanted my attention.

The argument began the evening I came home to find the television sitting on the piano, an open Coke can next to it. I had never lost my temper with Sarah, but that night something exploded in me. I picked up the TV and almost threw it to the floor, took the Coke and poured it down the sink, found a chamois and some lemon oil and began to carefully rub away the silver ring of water stain and the tiny scratches left by the TV. I was so angry it was difficult to look at her. For the first time, I raised my voice to her, demanding to know what she was thinking.

When she started to cry, it hurt my heart. I put down the chamois, gathered her in my arms and told her I was sorry.

She told me, between sobs, that she was sick of competing with a piano, that it was a big ugly freak that took up all the space and air and life in the living room. She told me it collected dust. She told me she was trying to make this our flat, but the piano insisted that it was only mine.

I held her and stroked her and murmured into her hair.

"I want you to get rid of the piano," she whispered.

I guided her to the bedroom. We made love *lento* this time, *doloroso*. When she fell asleep, I sat at the Bösendorfer, my fingers moving softly on her keys, pantomiming Mozart's *Concerto #20 in D Minor*, too sad to even cry.

I left early the next morning, before she awoke. I returned that night, anxious to put all this behind us, carrying roses and chocolates. She was happy for the presents, but she told me she meant it. I needed to dispose of the Bösendorfer this week, or she would leave me the next day. She would not be swayed.

I told her we could rearrange the flat to her liking. She said it would never work. I proposed we move. She said I was missing the point. I told her the Bösendorfer reminded me of Uncle Samuel. She said he was dead and she was very much alive. I said I didn't know how to get rid of a Bösendorfer. She suggested craigslist.

While Sarah sleeps, I tiptoe to the living room, put my fingers gently on those old ivory keys, lay my cheek on her soft sweet finish.

Three

Thea Constantine

Tribes

I felt guilty sometimes, spending the money Tommy and Willie tricked for. After all, I hadn't spent my time having my head pressed down over someone's stinking crotch, hadn't been fingered and groped in my most intimate places by some creepy stranger. I hadn't had to pretend I liked it, wanted it, was grateful for it.

I did love going out to breakfast with the boys though. Loved when they'd come swooping into whatever hole I happened to be in and pull me out of bed. Sometimes they'd dress me, fix my hair. Of all the girls, I was the smallest, the youngest, the easiest to talk into going out at ten a.m. dressed like Pippi Longstocking or Carmen Miranda. They'd go through my bags and pull out petticoats and scarves, hang all my bracelets on one skinny arm, and then we'd go to Arthur J's or the Snow White Cafe and eat our asses off. We were always starving.

They seemed to understand that I was just a little broken. Understood that there was no way I could ever make it in the straight world. They knew I could talk a good game and scam with the best of them, but my staying power was limited. If I wasn't in and out pretty fast, the whole thing would fall apart like Cinderella's carriage. My one attempt at getting a job in a phone room ended with me hyperventilating on Sunset Boulevard after only forty-five minutes.

We'd all met in San Francisco on Polk Street. Became part of the entourage headed by whoever had the power that week. I'd stroll up and down selling fake pills that I'd bought at Walgreens. They were made to look like real drugs, and I'd sell them as such. *BioSlim* were caffeine-loaded black capsules passing themselves off as black beauties. *Sleepinol* had the familiar *Tuinol* rainbow seal across the middle of the turquoise capsules. They were just a little bigger. In the dark of the clubs no one noticed. Ninety percent of the time my customers got so fucked up on whatever else they were taking, they never realized they weren't quite as fucked up as they should have been. The other ten percent of the time, I'd hide out 'til the person looking got tired.

We must have walked miles every evening up and down the same street. We'd pause to look in the window of the Palms, where people with day jobs sipped beautiful blue drinks in long frosted glasses, stop at the doughnut shop, where Tommy would shove day-olds on display into the hood of my pink sweater. Then we'd move on to the alcove where Bianca and the drag queens hung out and spend my beat pill money on the real thing.

Tommy and Willie were from Fresno. The girls and I were from Hollywood, my boyfriend, Michael, too. Bobby was from New York, Giasarra from Brazil. Blockhead and San Bruno (originally Sabrina) were from Arizona or New Mexico—I could never remember which.

In the summer the runaway population would double, and our numbers would grow, but the true core group were year-rounders. No one had parents in the traditional sense. Oh sure, there would be talk of someone's mom or sister, but otherwise there was little evidence. For the most part, the girls and I had the most middle-class backgrounds.

We did have family though. When Teri scored the apartment on Van Ness, we were over the moon. Empty as it was—it was ours at least for the month. It didn't stay empty long.

I remember furious rapping on the window and Troy running up all red-faced, asking for the keys to the front door. He and Tommy and Willie had managed to loot the lobby furniture from some B-grade hotel. A troop of boys began loading it in: huge gold lamps, an enormous gold and white sofa and two glass-topped occasional tables, one that still had a heavy chain around the base. Home is where the heart is.

The holidays were harder for those of us who'd once had them. When the only turkey with trimmings you ever got was provided by the state, you didn't miss it much. The first Thanksgiving, I got weepy. Memories of the family who no longer spoke to me ran in a loop, along with my vivid mental snapshots of meals gone by. You were supposed to be full on a day like this. Full of food, of comfort, of safety and warmth. Everyone else seemed fine with it, but I wasn't buying it as just another day like all the rest, which was how the girls told me to think of it. There were five of us in a cheap single room in the Leland, and all we had were a couple of boxes of Triscuits left over from when we grabbed a pallet of them off the back of a Nabisco truck weeks before. By that time, no one could stand the sight of the nasty little wheat squares. Someone suggested we could go to the mission, but that made me cry harder. I didn't want to be a sixteen-year-old bag lady. Going to the mission would mean that we weren't just having an adventure.

I guess they felt bad for me or maybe they were just sick of my whining. Someone went out and lifted a box of instant stuffing and a jar of gravy. Someone else came back with a couple of packets of cheap pressed turkey lunch meat and borrowed the electric skillet from the guy down the hall who Teri slept with from time to time. An onion appeared, some butter. A meal was cooked. I wish I could say I was as grateful as I should have been. I still feel bad that I didn't fuss over it like I should have.

We pinged up and down the coast—LA to San Francisco and back. We'd initially gone up to tend to our friend who fell climbing into a third story window high on angel dust. He'd broken his legs, his teeth had been smashed out along with a cheekbone. Until then he'd been one of the handsomest men I'd known. What we thought we could do for him, I don't know. Be there, I guess. It seemed very important that we stick together. He tried to run away when he first saw us. More like hobbled really, on his cane. It's so hard to lose your beauty. I didn't realize how hard back then.

When my boyfriend died, I fell apart. I'd just gone out with Giasarra to smoke a joint while he napped. Came back and saw there was a little drop of blood under his nose. I couldn't wake him up. I kept calling the ambulance, 911 or whatever they had then, but no one came for forty-five minutes. When the paramedics finally showed up, they pronounced him DOA. Said it was because of the half-life of some of the pills we were taking, the ones that were supposed to get us off another drug. They stay inside you, or half of them do. Then they sealed off our room leaving me on the street half hysterical. I don't know who spotted me and spread the word, but the girls came and got me, took me to their room. I think I was in shock. I'd only had one close friend die on me so far. Why him and not me? My memories of that time are dreamlike. I just remember a big room with a bed where I lay and people came and sat with me. Brought me little gifts, drugs and candy and knick-knacks. It was what I needed. I don't remember how long I stayed there or when I first got out of bed. They walked me back up and down the street again. I got stronger.

Things change, people don't. That's what Bobby used to say. I think of Shelly. She lived in a room upstairs from us at the Leland. She invited Teri and me up one time to do our nails. We thought she was a drag queen, but it turned out she was in the middle of the full-on change. She had all these nail polishes. Every color. I think she felt she had to lure us up with something nice —but we really liked her. She wanted to experience girl talk, female bonding or something. We learned a lot about what they call gender re-assignment now. She was having it done at Stanford. She owned a really nice restaurant and had a house somewhere, but she'd moved into the city for the duration of her change. They made her wait a really long time. She said she'd gone through tons of psychological and physical tests. Stanford wouldn't do it unless you had a certain amount of female organs. Turns out a lot of us have all kinds of little surprises lurking around inside. She was on hormones and so far, they'd done her breasts.

One of the things I loved about Teri is that she'd ask the questions you wanted to ask but were too polite or scared to. She asked if we could see Shelly's new breasts. If we could touch them. They were perfect and they felt so smooth but a little hard too. The biggest surprise, though, was the ship tattooed across them. A huge one, with sails and masts, the whole nine yards. Like the kind people put in bottles. She'd really tried hard to be a man at one time. Tried so hard she joined the navy and got married, had a couple kids. I asked if she wanted to get rid of it, like a painful memory, but she didn't want to. It was a part of her journey, the scars she carried. We were always tempted to ask her to take us to her restaurant for something to eat but we didn't. I'm surprised sometimes when I think of the times we held back. Why this and not that?

Shelly had a happy ending I think. I saw her months later walking with some friends. She'd had the whole operation by then. She was wearing a little cardigan and a tweedy skirt. Her friends were dressed the same as she was. Very low key. We chatted for a bit, moved on. I imagined the fanciful ship sailing beneath her twin set. The little surprises you don't see.

We all had scars, the kind you could see. Tommy ended up with a huge one that went from his navel up to his chest. A pink shiny dividing line, thick and brutal. Willy had a split eyebrow that looked like a lightning bolt. We acquired the roundish divots from abscesses, the ones that look like tiny meteors landed on your arms. Those and the telltale lines that traced our veins like maps of our circulatory systems. Our friend who fell out the window had what looked like laugh lines that radiated out from his eyes, but they were scars. He had big ones on his legs, too, with stitch marks you could see. Teri had them on her wrists. I had one across my throat. It's hard to lose your beauty, but it's part of the journey I guess. I'm married to a man with one across his lips. It was one of the ways I could tell he was for me.

Mary Mandeville

Messages

On the Monday before Thanksgiving, my sister Joan called with news the doctor had just given her. He said treatment was failing, said there were new tumors, said neither scalpel nor cyber-knife had done their jobs, said all the rocks on this damned rocky road have been turned over. He said get your affairs in order, Joan, you have about four weeks left.

The ache beneath my breastbone threatened to split me open. How long is four weeks? How short?

"I'm worried about Ally." Joan spoke of her six-year-old daughter in a whisper.

"She'll be okay." I stated it like a complete certainty though I still felt that cracking sensation in my chest. Of course she worried about the daughter she adopted all alone.

"Maybe it's better this way." Joan's voice turned thick.

We'd had variations of this conversation before, this idea of Joan's that her cancer was a divine plan hatched to move her daughter to a "better" family of a mom and dad and two sisters instead of a single mother. The number of reservations I had about my youngest sister and her husband as Ally's future parents was zero, but it broke my heart to hear Joan contemplate this line of thinking again. I put a hand over my mouth so she wouldn't hear me sniffle.

"Maybe she'll have a better life with Susan and Brad." As her words trembled, I knew tears had begun to fall.

"Look," I said, my voice big-sister firm, "you didn't get cancer so Ally would go to a new home." There were a thousand possible culprits behind the aggressive breast cancer, but the disruption of a little girl's mother-daughter relationship wasn't one of them. "She'll be happy before too long." I swallowed to keep my own voice from trembling. "But *you* are the one who gave her a great start in life."

"I'm thinking of making some videotapes for her." She got the words out through sniffles and gulps.

"Brilliant."

We talked through our sorrow about what Joan might say on the tapes for her only child, about who would take care of her dog, about why the hell she got such a lousy, life-sucking cancer.

Where would she go? Would all her old dearly departed dogs be waiting, tails wagging, to greet her when she stepped onto some celestial field? Would she meet Dad, Grandma, Grandpa? Would she be born again to live another life—say in Ireland or Tibet? Would she come back as one of the German shepherds she loved?

"I hope you'll send me a sign from wherever you are." I wanted her to remember me, to keep in touch with me, as if this dying thing couldn't separate us.

"I'll do my best." Giant sigh. "I don't know what my messaging capabilities will be."

I couldn't stifle a laugh. My little sister, the telecommunications CEO and gadget girl. I bet she had major concerns about her upcoming 'messaging capabilities.'

Later, I worried. Had I said everything I needed to say?

In four weeks it would be Christmas. Though our time together hadn't yet run out, I wanted more. *Just Christmas,* I prayed a little to the bearded old white-man God of my childhood but mostly to a vague Divine I hoped like hell was listening. *Can she at least live till Christmas?*

I called my mother, my brothers, my youngest sister. Together we whispered, cried, and wondered aloud: What do you get a dying person for Christmas?

Then a friend made a suggestion.

Give her messages, she said.

Messages?

Yes, she said. *Every thought you ever wished you'd told her, or don't want to regret not telling her. All of them. You have the chance. Write them down.*

When my friend's rabbi died, members of the synagogue bought stacks of colored origami paper. Everyone interested wrote messages for the family on those little squares. Then they folded them into Stars of David, pinned them to a large picture board, and presented them to his grieving loved ones. My friend wished they'd been able to present messages to the rabbi himself before he died.

This was the solution to the Christmas present dilemma. But how would I sell it to the whole family? My youngest sister, Susan, would be on board, sensitive, emotional, and communicative. My youngest brother, Tom, with his bent toward the expressive, would probably sign on. Our other brothers, practical, hard-working men, might find it too squishy and touchy-feely. I broached the subject anyway over long-distance phone calls.

They surprised me. *Yes,* said Bud, a civil engineer who hides his sensitive side under a terse and prickly exterior. *That's a great idea. Paula and the kids will like it, too. Yes,* said John, a never-married accountant who works for the IRS, *I'll be glad to. Yes,* said Joe, a nuclear physicist who spends much time in the research lab and recently married Emiri, a brainy neurosurgeon from Japan.

We decided to pitch in on a fancy high-tech video camera as well, so she could make those tapes for Ally. The paper messages would be a Christmas present—fingers crossed—but the video camera needed to be ASAP. Thanksgiving. Pronto. My brothers would research and purchase the camera; we'd all get started on the handwritten messages.

Squares of crisp origami paper in all colors of the rainbow would soon be covered with messages to Joan. But how should we present them? Fold them into stars? Christmas ornaments? Hearts?

A message came via Facebook from my new sister-in-law, Emiri.

I'll fold them into cranes.

That's perfect, I thought. *Well, I guess you know how. To fold paper cranes, I mean. Could you? It's not too much?*

I could. I will.

At their mention, I wanted paper cranes and wanted them bad. The desire reverberated, touching something bigger than Joan and her individual cancer, bigger than our not-so-small family, bigger than us and our problems, offering hope where there hadn't been any. My paper crane longing became a chord vibrating beneath my solar plexus. I was reminded of the endangered whooping cranes I watched lift off the ground at a sanctuary in Wisconsin, their decimated numbers gradually growing again; of Sadako, the Japanese girl immortalized in a book. Sick with leukemia because of radiation exposure from the atomic bomb dropped in Hiroshima, Sadako set to work making cranes.

Folding paper cranes for good fortune dated back to an ancient Japanese legend about cranes who were said to have lived a thousand years. Each folded crane became a wish for healing, long life, best of luck. One folded crane, one wish; one thousand cranes, a most special wish. Sadako tried to fold a thousand cranes before she died, an act of optimistic defiance in the face of waning hope.

I wanted cranes for Joan, and for all of us. Not the legendary thousand cranes—there was obviously not time for that—just enough to carry our messages. But it might be exploitive to load the task onto our newest family member just because she could fold them.

There might be a lot.

Emiri smiled at me over Facebook. *I can do it. :-)*

Seriously, it could be as many as fifty. I was doing the math on the time it might take: six siblings and mom, assorted spouses and kids, aunts and uncles; with two or three messages per person it would add up to forty or fifty pieces of paper, and to fold, what—twenty minutes per crane? That's like a thousand minutes.

Not a problem. :-)

And so it was agreed.

At home in Portland, Oregon, my partner and I and our two sons sat around the dining room table. The boys surprised me, the way they dove into the task, writing some messages and drawing others. With minimal talk, we each accumulated a small pile of tie-dyed origami squares, as if we hoped if we wrote enough or drew enough, we could change what was happening.

You welcomed me into the family.

You came to my adoption ceremony.

You've been an awesome mother. Ally's been blessed to have you.

Best. Sister. Ever.

We stuffed our scrawled origami messages into envelopes. Joined by other notes, scribbled by five-year-olds and eighty-year-olds and even sulky teenagers, from us in Oregon and others in Washington, Idaho, and Montana, they soared across the country to Emiri in Boston, carrying a rainbow of sentiments on their papery wings.

How's it going? I Facebook-messaged my sister-in-law. Our little family of four had sent off more than twenty messages, and I worried that with all the others, there might be too many.

Don't worry. I can do it.

A couple weeks later I walked into Joan's house. She'd made it to Christmas (maybe someone in heaven listened to my prayers after all). I wanted to look into the eyes made lopsided by a tumor and take stock of my sister's heart. Before I could, the sight of a four-foot mobile, its many multicolored paper strands swirling in the breeze created by the open door, stopped me in the entry hall.

"Whoa." I don't know what I'd pictured, a bag maybe, or a box, or a pile of folded cranes, perhaps. Not this huge, surprising whirligig.

Emiri slipped to my side and greeted me with a small bow of head and shoulders. I reached my fingers out to touch the delicate paper structure. "It's so many."

"It's a thousand." Emiri's husband, my brother Joe, stood beside her with his arm around her shoulder, a broad beam lighting up his face. "I tried to help, but I folded about three for every hundred of hers."

My eyes moved between Joe and Emiri. The sides of my throat squeezed together and caught my words on their way out. Emiri pressed her palms together, smiled, then closed her eyes and bowed again, more deeply this time. I bent at the waist, wanted to touch my fingers to the floor to show my thanks; instead, a simple lean and drop of chin to chest. "It's beautiful. Thank you."

"It has to be a thousand, you know."

I did know.

My ten-year-old son pushed open the entry door I'd closed behind me. It was ten degrees on the side of Mt. Jumbo in Rattlesnake Canyon just outside Missoula, Montana. The rush of frigid air pushed the mobile and the paper birds fluttered in a semblance of flight. Our messages had flown cross-country and back and now each colorful crane danced in the cold. The whole mobile spun on its string axis.

One thousand paper cranes.

❖   ❖   ❖

Christmas was the last time I saw Joan as my fully functioning sister. I understood then it wasn't Christmas that mattered, it was time with Joan. Our paper messages provided a way for us to accept the unacceptable and to celebrate and honor our sister before she left us forever. We wanted Valentine's Day and Spring Equinox and Easter too, but what we got was Christmas and cranes.

Mom told me Joan took apart the message cranes—Emiri had made 'message strands' that could be snipped from the mobile leaving the rest intact—and read them on freezing Montana winter days. When the buttons on her smart phone overwhelmed her and the function of the remote control became baffling, our simple print on paper reached her. By the time I saw her at the end of January, cancer was eating her brain and she didn't remember. By the end of February, she was gone.

After she died, my mother, brothers, younger sister and I, each in our own time, read the thoughts that lingered on featherweight origami squares. It helped us weather those first post-Joan weeks. Unable to avoid losing someone cherished, we could at least hold her—and each other—with our words. The sentiments we shared became a way of joining hands to walk with someone we loved to a gate we could not pass through.

One piece of pink paper had these printed words: *You never let me down. Not once. Not ever.* My fingers flew to my lips when I read it.

"Do you know who wrote this, Mom?" I walked across the shiny wood floor from the dining table to where Mom sat sipping coffee in the breakfast nook and placed the wisp of paper in front of her.

"I thought maybe you did." She thought for a moment. "But it could have been John."

"Or Susan," I said, but then thought maybe it was a niece or nephew instead. "Or Chris or Rachel."

Mom took another swallow from her mug. "It could have been anyone."

My sister must still be working out her messaging capabilities because I haven't heard from her in the crystal clear way I hoped. I admit to wishing for a message on my smart phone—a text I couldn't otherwise explain or some crazy technical malfunction that I'd believe was from her. The appearance on my doorstep of a stray German shepherd would do it, too.

I've survived difficulty before: the death of my father, the fracture of a long-term relationship, the passing of friends. Somehow, even through the densest sorrow, my heart kept on beating. What I hadn't realized before Joan's death and the cranes is that a grieving heart is capable of soaring. I know because mine did, with the strength of a thousand pairs of wings.

That message from my sister? Only time will tell. But she never let me down in life. Not once. Not ever.

So I can wait.

Nikki Schulak

Vulvar Fantasy

How often do you look at your vulva? I'll bet you can't remember the last time. Let's face it. Examining your vulva is awkward. It takes creativity, and also a level of privacy that a mother with two young children is rarely afforded. Besides, there aren't a lot of reasons to look at your vulva unless 1) you're into that sort of thing, or 2) it itches, and you think it might be cancer.

My gynecologist handed me a mirror and took me on a little vulvar tour.

"Are you comfortable, Nikki? Can you see everything alright?"

"I can."

"Can you see this?"

"Yes."

"This is the area that concerns me. This darkened area just above the perineum region." She points with the soft end of a Q-tip. "I'd like to do a biopsy."

I hate it when doctors are concerned.

"Don't worry. I'm just going to take a bit of tissue from here—and here." She places emphasis with the Q-tip. "But not from here." She points to a porcelain-colored spot, which also, apparently, concerns her. "That's too close to your clitoris."

Ah, my clitoris.

"I'll give you two shots of Lidocaine. They'll feel like bee stings. After that you shouldn't feel a thing."

Oh, ouch.

I'd been itching for a few months when I made the appointment. No one is saying I have cancer.

The doctor suspects a skin disease called lichen sclerosis. But she also uses the words *melanoma* and *squamous cells*. I hear her distinctly. She tells me when

I read the lab report on My Chart not to panic if I see the words *melanoma* or *squamous cells*. My Chart is the new program adopted by the university hospital that makes it possible for patients to check their own lab reports online.

At the moment, I'm not panicked about anything except the impending vulvar bee stings.

Shelly the nurse enters to prep the room for my biopsy. She dons purple gloves and pours Betadine into a shallow, kidney-shaped, stainless steel bowl. Shelly has inch-long bleached blond hair. She sends me off to provide a urine sample. This is difficult because the toilet is an automatic flusher. Every time I try to gather some urine, the toilet flushes, forcing me to stop peeing and pull the sample cup to safety. I figure this must be a test. I pass the test and return triumphantly with my sample. Shelly has set up a series of sharp instruments on a tray. She's removing her gloves. "Now don't you worry a minute about the biopsy. Dr. Mason does these every day. She's really awesome."

Why does everyone keep telling me not to worry?

Shelly is a nominee for Best Nurse of the Year Award. I know this because she's wearing an addendum on her nametag that says so. "Look." Shelly pulls her white tights taut against her skin to reveal a brightly colored tattoo of a shooting star. It covers half her calf. "Now *this* really *hurt*," she says matter-of-factly. "The tattooist said it would feel like sandpaper rubbed over a burn, over and over again—and it did. It felt just like that." She tells me this in a conspiratorial whisper. Shelly pauses and looks me over. I'm wrapped in a paper sheet holding a sample cup full of urine. "Do you have any tattoos?" she asks, no longer whispering. I shake my head modestly.

My mind wanders as I climb back up on the table. I'm thinking about pain. I'm thinking about vulvar tattoos. This is a good distraction. Do people get vulvar tattoos? Sure they do. There's nothing people don't do. The print on the wall of the exam room is titled "Asian Pear." A pear-like fruit has been sliced in half and set on a silk cloth. The cut fruit looks like female anatomy. How subtle. My doctor returns. She's a tiny woman with big, curly hair. She totters confidently on three-inch heels. The toes of her shoes are very pointy. Shelly asks if I want her to hold my hand. "Thanks," I reply. "I'd rather just hold on to the edge of this table here and cringe."

Dr. Mason tells me to breathe.

It turns out that the bee stings and the biopsies both hurt, but the bee stings hurt more. They make me swear like a rap star. Why can't they skip the shots and just do the biopsies? Even my dentist gives me laughing gas. When the procedure is over, Dr. Mason extends the hand mirror toward me. "Would you like to see what I've done?"

I don't. I just want to go home and never look at my vulva again.

I waddle around in the afternoon and evening. The anesthesia wears off and I am sore. My husband is out of town for a week so I rent six chick flicks; I plan to watch one each evening after the kids are asleep. The first night my daughter wakes in the middle of *Juno*. She's had a nightmare. "I dreamed Daddy never came home," she says simply. I crawl in bed with her. In the morning, I get my kids to school. Then, I call my friend Cassie to tell her about my biopsies.

"Are you scared? Do you think you have cancer? Did you read that book I told you about, *Crazy, Sexy, Cancer*?"

I still haven't read the book.

"I'm not *scared,* exactly. I'm a little worried. What if Ben's plane crashes and I have cancer? Who will take care of our kids?"

My mother's mother died from colon cancer when my mother was nine. My mother died from breast cancer when I was twenty-eight. We have a small cancer legacy going on in my family. It's indulgent, I know, but whenever I have a physical anomaly, I always assume the worst.

"I'll think good thoughts about your vulva," Cassie promises. "I'll make a pastel of your vulva. I'll make an altar to your vulva. I'll pray on it."

Dr. Mason has said she'll post the results of my biopsies on My Chart in about a week, and also call me. Waiting is hard. I can't resist checking My Chart two nights later, right after watching *27 Dresses*. No results yet.

My Chart is a theoretically practical concept. I log on to the website and enter a password; suddenly, here's my medical history managed by some stranger who apparently knows my vulva itches. I can see my current height and weight. I'm reminded that I have an allergy to egg whites, and a prescription for Ambien. I have a family history of stroke, heart disease, diabetes—and, of course, cancer. Also, I note that I have something called tinea.

What the heck is tinea? I Google it. Tinea is ringworm. Please note: it's a fungus, not actually a worm. But it is contagious. *I've never had ringworm!* I'm indignant.

The stranger who's entered this information has obviously made a mistake. Or maybe it's a joke. More likely it's a mistake. My medical information has been switched with somebody else's. Some poor sap out there is reviewing his own My Chart page wondering when exactly he had a bout of vulvar itching. Doubt has now been cast on the validity and accuracy of the entire My Chart program. I do some additional research about ringworm. Maybe I had it but I forgot? I look at images of ringworm. I would remember if I'd had that. But, wait, this image does look familiar! This image looks exactly like . . . the red splotch on my husband's upper thigh. I call him right away even though it's 3 a.m. in New Jersey. I leave a message on his cell phone. "I think you gave me ringworm. I think I have vulvar ringworm."

The next afternoon a neighbor invites me and my kids for a bike ride.

"I can't." I whisper to her about my biopsies.

"Oh," she whispers back and nods knowingly. "Vulvular problems?"

"Vulvar problems."

"Oh, yes?" Her eyes widen slightly.

"It's vulvar. Not vul*v*ular."

"Are you sure? Vulvar doesn't sound right."

"The nurse kept saying *vulvar*. I thought it sounded wrong, too. But I looked it up and it's definitely vulvar."

"Oh, yeah. Like how people mispronounce *nu-cue-ler*." She smiles at me.

"*Vul-var. Vul-var.*" She keeps repeating the word like she doesn't want to forget it.

"Vulvar. Yep."

"Remember that *Seinfeld* episode where Jerry dates a girl whose name rhymes with vulva? Mulva or something? Or, no wait. Was it De-LOR-es? Rhymes with cli-TOR-is?"

"Right. I think it was De-LOR-es," I say. When will this conversation come to a natural end?

"So do you have VD? Or something more serious?"

That night I watch *Knocked Up*. Then I study images of lichen sclerosis on the

Internet. Because I read that women with scarring from lichen sclerosis are at higher risk for vulvar cancer, I look at pictures of vulvar cancer, too. These are disturbing images. The opposite of erotica. People don't whisper the cancer word as softly as they used to, but I wonder how folks respond when told that someone has vulvar cancer. You give condolences, sure, but questions hang in the air: Do they remove vulvas? Can you still have sex? What about your clitoris?

What happens to your clitoris?

I call my friend Stella. She's a midwife and lives in Madison, Wisconsin. She counseled me through my failed attempt to breastfeed my adopted daughter. She listens patiently as I talk about my worries. "Know what you need, honey? You need a Wondrous Vulva Puppet.[1] I just bought one for Allison." Allison is her eleven-year-old. Her older daughter, Claire, is sixteen. "I have a vulva puppet in my office, but I wanted Allison to have her own."

"Did you buy a puppet for Claire, too?"

"Claire doesn't need one. She's got her own, hard-working vulva. And a gorgeous boyfriend who practically lives at our house."

"Does this boyfriend sleep in Claire's room?"

"Yes."

"And you're okay with that?"

"Honey, I grew up thinking sex was dirty. I never want my daughters to have sex in the back of a car because they don't have a place to go. I never want Claire to have sex and then come home feeling like she's got to hide the fact that she's a sexual being or that she's dirty or bad. I want her to be able to have sex in her own room, in her own bed, if she wants to."

"What do you tell Allison when . . . what's his name?"

"Jim."

"When Jim comes out of Claire's room in the morning?"

Stella's quiet for a moment. "Jim sleeps on the couch."

"Jim and Claire have sex in Claire's room, then Jim sleeps on the couch?"

"No, that's just what I tell Allison. I tell her Jim sleeps on the couch."

I promise Stella I'll look at the vulva puppets, and I do. These vulvas are luscious in colorful velvet and silk. Each puppet is adorned with glass beads. Even better, they're made in a fair-trade co-op in a shantytown in Lima, Peru. From the puppet site you can link to The Vulva Sisters singing "Do the Kegel." I call Cassie and tell her about the puppets. Then I call Marian. She's my friend who's most recently had breast cancer. It was a small lump, but an aggressive cancer. She chose to have a prophylactic double mastectomy.

"What are you afraid of, Nikki?" She knows my fears.

"I don't want to lose my vulva." I don't mean to sound whiny.

"You're jumping way ahead of yourself, Nikki. You're going to be just fine."

Marian reminds me that when her aunt had a hysterectomy, she knitted her a uterus. She asks if I'd like her to knit me a vulva. I do. I want a bright purple, mohair vulva. She says she'll get right on it.

If I were going blind, I'd make a point to see the world—the Grand Canyon, the Northern Lights.

If I were going deaf, I'd listen for hours to spring peepers, thunderstorms, my children's voices.

And if I were told I needed a vulvectomy and a clitoridectomy, would I have as much sex as possible? Absolutely. I would preserve my orgasms in jars like peaches in summer. If you read the gynecological cancer literature, the counselors try to make you feel better by saying things like, "Sex isn't just about the act of sex. You can pleasure your partner through gentle snuggling, sharing a movie together, or planning a special meal." I hope it never comes to that. I value snuggling and watching movies with my husband. But I don't want to replace fucking with movie night. Of course, I'd rather be alive than dead with my clitoris intact. But still.

I watch *Waitress*. Then I study a website that features intricately made velvet vulva purses.[2] Each purse has a sumptuous fabric labia and a beautiful button clitoris. Some of them are machine washable. If I could afford it, I'd send one to every woman I love.

Cassie calls. She's just driven two seventh graders home from school. They were fresh from sex education.

"The vulva puppet was gross! The teacher held it up to her own vulva and, you know, touched it!"

"She put her fingers in it and told us we should touch our own vulvas!"

Cassie can't believe it. Neither can I. Suddenly everyone we know is talking about vulva puppets. It's a vulva puppet convergence. "I think it's a good sign," Cassie says. "Have you heard from your doctor?"

[1] *www.yoni.com/vulvas/holidayvulvas.html*

[2] *www.artgoddess.com/purses.html*

❖   ❖   ❖

A week after the biopsy, nothing new is posted on My Chart. I call the office and speak to the nurse. The results are in.

"Please read them."

"It says here the first patch is suspect lichen sclerosis."

"Oh." I feel immediate relief. It's not cancer.

"And the second patch is also suspect lichen sclerosis."

"That's good." I guess it's good. It could be a lot worse. At least I'll be able to report back to my neighbor that I don't have VD. I give the nurse a list of questions for my doctor. She promises to call me with more information.

I am at the playground with my dog and my two kids when the nurse calls back. It's noisy but I tell her to go ahead.

"First of all, I have to apologize. I misread your lab report." My dog is barking and my kids are arguing so I'm pretty sure I haven't heard her correctly.

"What? Can you speak up?"

"I'm sorry, but I misread your lab."

"You misread my lab?"

"Yes. I'm really sorry." I move to a quieter area under a tree. "I accidentally read you the doctor's notes—the notes she'd written to the pathologist when she sent your biopsies out. She suspected lichen sclerosis, but the pathologist doesn't.

She Holds the Face of the World

His report is actually inconclusive."

"What do you mean?"

"The report didn't come back conclusive for anything. But Dr. Mason wants to treat your vulva as if you have lichen sclerosis. She's called in a prescription for a steroid cream. And we need to schedule you for a follow-up."

You know how some women don't tell anyone they're pregnant during the first trimester, just in case? Now that my biopsy is "inconclusive" I don't want to keep talking about it. But my friends call. I tell them I have ringworm.

My yoga teacher says, "We have to be in this body for the rest of our lives." You get to a certain age and you start knowing peers who have cancer, first one, then another, and it slowly dawns on you, this is the beginning of the end. You might live another forty or fifty years. But chances are, you won't.

The best movie I watch during my week of vulvar fantasy is *The Heartbreak Kid*. I especially like the scene where Malin Akerman pees on Ben Stiller after he's attacked by a Portuguese man-o'-war. And the best vulvar product I learn about isn't a puppet or a purse. It's Vulva, the perfume. Vulva isn't actually a perfume but rather "the erotic, intimate scent of an irresistible woman." I don't need to add to the clever commentary that's already been written about Vulva, but I will. Despite the fact that the URL for Vulva is www.smellmeand.com, do not mistake this web page for pornography. The models are naked, their vulvas are hairless, but I think they're mocking Vulva. Even the lady who's about to receive oral stimulation in an Eames chair seems, at best, amused. The woman who provides the site's voice-over reads the copy in a deep alto with a thick German accent. I just love hearing her say "beguiling vaginal scent." I play it over and over until I laugh so hard I cry.

Heather Durham

Ablaze

"You have too much fire," my acupuncturist announces, reading the signs. My flushed face, burgundy tongue, rapid, jittery pulse. I pull off my shirt and lie face down on the soft cotton sheets of the treatment table. Lightning quick, she flicks tiny needles into my skin. Pinpricks of electricity zing the top of my head, back of my neck, along both sides of my spine. Then the webbing between thumb and forefinger, and the space between ankle and Achilles. She lays a cool hand on the small of my back and breathes, "Rest. I'll be back later." I exhale deeply, savoring this pleasure on the knife-edge of pain.

When I was small my father taught me to extinguish candles with bare fingers. I learned young to reach for flame.

A childhood of summers spent at sleep-away camp sparked an affection for the dry snap crackle of campfires. Eastern white pine, red oak, and paper birch. Charred marshmallows and crispy black-skinned hotdogs. Sitting cross-legged on pine needles, I leaned toward the flames, staring, as if determining whether friend or foe. The bold scarlets and ochres drew me in; the elusive cobalts and violets kept me there. Unable to look away, though my eyes burned.

There were other fires of childhood, stoked by a father who hit a mother. By a mother who wailed. By nights spent wide awake willing myself not to listen to the screaming. Acid burned in the pit of my stomach.

When I was five I shattered the glass of the front door with my fist. I wanted out.

Eighteen years later, when I did get out, fire stayed with me. I moved west, found the incense smoke of juniper, fir, and cedar. Wild singing fires, ardent laughing fires, and fervent naked dancing fires. Outdoor school naturalist fires I arranged with my own hands, then lit and supervised as if they were unruly children. And the cleansing fires of prescribed burns.

Adulthood ignited other flames. Sensual heat of skin on skin. Men. Women. Spring fevers, summer passions, fall restlessness, and winter smolderings.

I learned to create fire without matches. That with the right fuel and fortitude, friction transforms wood into smoking black dust, a dust that when added to tinder, I could blow into flame. The combustion of my own breath.

With creation came destruction.

Mysterious hives, inflamed joints, explosive anger, mania. A searing rage I tried to cut out of me with razors and shards of glass. The same burn drove me into tattoo studios to endure hours of needles drilling colors into skin. Inky flames forever on my back.

I watched a fuming father drown in whiskey. Saw the spark go out in his eyes. His heart. His body. Until he was extinguished.

Not everyone can take the heat. But I learned young to reach for flame.

I fanned my own fire. I stalked it, moved wherever it led me. Zigzagging across the country, I zip-lined off bridges in New Hampshire, banded raptors in Nevada, tended bobcats in Florida, massaged at a hot springs commune in Oregon, taught fire ecology in the Colorado Rockies, and learned wilderness survival in Washington.

I sought out the cleansing fire of a New Year's ceremony, a community bonfire fed with offerings and prayers. The leader raked the daylong fire into glowing coals as twilight advanced. That frozen day, too clear and cold to snow, I removed boots and wool socks, rolled up pants, scrunched up long underwear, and stepped toward the glow. Then walked calmly, almost floating, onto the coals. I felt only a tingling ache in my toes and the ecstasy of a phoenix resurrected from her own ashes. My feet turned black, but did not burn. The key is to keep moving.

She comes to take the needles out. Flicks them out of my feet, hands, back, neck, and head. I sit up and pull on my shirt, breathing evenly. Calm for now. She tells me to go easy on spicy food, beating sun, scalding baths. To avoid stressful situations. I smile and say nothing.

I will always reach for flame. The ache on the knife-edge of ecstasy. There is no other way. There is no such thing as too much fire.

Patty Somlo

Quality Courts

My dad is sitting on the edge of the bed, staring at the TV. I'm sitting on the edge of the other double bed, close to the door. The bedspread has a rough synthetic feel. Orange and turquoise designs swirl across the brown background in an attempt, I imagine, at cheerfulness.

I've come to this motel room in the heart of Fisherman's Wharf to talk to my dad. I'm studying his left ear and the loose skin on his neck. He's completely absorbed in the game.

When I was a kid, motel rooms like this made me feel gloomy.

Thirty years later, nothing has changed.

Most people grow up in houses. Me, I grew up in motel rooms. And cheap military housing that looked like motels, except the furniture wasn't as cheerful.

My mother, a wavy-haired brunette who never left home without a fresh coat of Revlon Love That Red staining her lips, served as our family's motel analyst. In a squishy white leather purse that resembled an unroasted marshmallow, she guarded a fat small book. She studied it as we rode in the Dodge or the Plymouth—we never owned a Ford or a Chevrolet—on interminable rides whose sole destination was the next motel room. We were allowed to stay only at places listed in the book, *Quality Courts,* motels touted to be safe and clean, owned by people with high moral standards. Otherwise, we could catch something from the toilet.

My dad hasn't taken his eyes off the television screen the whole time I've been here. He came all the way across country from San Antonio, to sit in this motel room at Fisherman's Wharf and watch TV. The trip took five days by train. He will be here for two. Then he'll hop back on the train for the return five-day ride.

When I was a kid, my sisters and I made up car games to pass the time as we rode for miles past fields dotted with cows and cornfields and even fields of tall cactus. We played license plate games, counted cars and read billboards. Sometimes we'd sing a string of Broadway show tunes. If I think about my family, I picture them in their designated seats: Dad in the driver's seat, his black hair combed smooth up and away from his forehead, the gold-rimmed aviator sunglasses he wore with his khaki green flight jacket hiding his eyes; Mom in the passenger seat, her arms bare in a sleeveless cotton dress, blowing smoke from her L&M cigarette out the small triangular side window; and my sisters, one dark and one blond, on either side of me in the back. Being the youngest, I got sandwiched in the middle of car seats and single beds pushed together.

We traveled in the fifties and early sixties, when the highway consisted of only two lanes. Motels, restaurants and hand-painted signs appeared alongside the road. The Quality Courts my mother selected were painted bright pink or aquamarine, like houses in Mexico, with single-story rooms strung like pearls around the pool or miniature golf course or little playground. Pudgy glasses wrapped in thick plastic that crackled when you took it off sat on thin glass shelves over the toilet beside white buckets for ice. Cokes from the machine next to the motel office came in cold green glass bottles.

Three weeks before my dad boarded the train in San Antonio, I got a note from him. "We'll be in San Francisco 5/8–5/10. Hope to see you," the note said. It had been nearly four years since I had seen my dad. The last time was because my oldest sister, Barbara, had suddenly died.

As it happens, today is the one day I have to spend with my father and only until about 2:00 o'clock. I can almost hear the meter ticking. It's 10:30 already. The game has moved into the third quarter, the announcer just said, and my dad wants to see how it's going to end.

I always wanted to stay in a motel with a swimming pool. Otherwise the nights would be as dreary as the days. The motels with swimming pools were more expensive, though. If I got lucky, the only Quality Court within a hundred-mile radius from our destination would have a pool. Then, we'd have no choice.

Before my mother picked out the place we would stay each night, I would borrow the book from her and send my eyes flying down the column labeled P. I didn't care about the other columns—T for television, A for air conditioning, and R for restaurant. A star under P meant a reprieve from my life breathing in smoke exhaled by my parents in the front seat as I watched the road signs pass by. A star promised me hours of practicing the breast stroke before dark and perfecting my Esther Williams imitation, furiously scooping up water with my hands to lower my body while my stiff right leg and toes pointed skyward.

During the commercials, my dad turns around on the bed to talk to me. He gives me the names and locations of restaurants I should try the next time I'm in Paris. My father doesn't ask if I plan to visit Paris anytime soon. My entire adult life has been spent on the frayed edge of frugality. In the sixties and seventies, I traveled by bumming rides and staying in Mexican motels that would have had my mother chasing after me from the grave, her hands filled with Handi Wipes and room deodorizer. My father assumes my world still revolves around the world, as it did when I was a child.

One of my clearest memories is of my father coming home from trips. I remember sitting on the worn green carpet of our duplex at Hickam Air Force Base in Hawaii watching my father, in his pressed tan cotton uniform with the short sleeves, unzipping his green nylon flight bag. I can picture him pulling out the presents he brought me back from Japan. A pink silk scarf with snow-covered Mt. Fujiyama in the center. A Japanese doll dressed in a red brocade kimono in a black-framed glass case. A shiny lacquered jewelry box with a mirror inside and the outline of Mt. Fujiyama painted on it.

Every half hour, my father sniffs from one of several pastel-colored inhalers. He takes pills from bottles lined up along the dresser. Since the last time I saw him, my father has shrunken into a frail old man.

For the third time, my dad tells me about a trip he and his wife took last year to Alaska. Of all the places he has been, Alaska is his favorite. Riding in the tour bus, he passed caribou herds grazing alongside the road. In his old age, my father feels a sense of awe about life I don't recall him ever having.

When I was a child, we moved on the average of once every two years and sometimes every year. The packers came one day. The movers came the next. The morning after the movers lifted the last piece of our furniture into the van, the five of us would hop into our designated seats in the car.

We had an ETD, an estimated time of departure, and an ETA, an estimated time of arrival. The ETD always occurred when it was still dark, before the crack of dawn, around 0500 hours. The ETA was never before 1700 hours at night.

During the trip, we ate breakfast in the motel room: packaged powdered-sugar donuts that stuck to the roof of my mouth, washed down with pineapple juice that came in small cans and had a strong metallic aftertaste and a strange fishy smell. We ate sandwiches at the rest area picnic tables along the side of the road, baloney or ham on white bread with mustard, never mayonnaise, because mayonnaise would spoil in the heat.

Twenty years have passed since my father retired from the Air Force. But he is still traveling. Each year, he and his wife send for brochures about trips to Australia or Portugal, cruises to Alaska, or African safaris. My father keeps searching for a place he has never been. He has come to San Francisco, I learn, because he had never ridden the train before. This seemed the perfect time to do so.

On our travels across country, I collected glass horses. Whenever we made a bathroom stop, I would scout out the nearest souvenir shop and search for a horse I didn't already have. I especially liked it when I found a family with three or four horses that looked exactly alike, except they got progressively tinier.

After every move, I would hold my breath when I unpacked. Before long, I understood that if the newspaper felt loose, a horse had gotten shattered. My mother would assure me that we could glue the broken horse back together. I knew she was wrong. Gluing would make it last for a time but it would eventually crumble into pieces worthless as dust.

I try talking to my father about my life, about my work, and about the graduate program I am finishing. Each time I try, he changes the subject, turning it back on himself. When I was in my twenties, I took my boyfriend, Phil, to San Antonio for a weeklong visit with my dad. At the end of the visit, Phil said to me, "You know, if your dad was a stranger I sat next to on a train, I would find him fascinating. But he's your dad. He doesn't talk to you like he knows you. He talks to you like you're some stranger on a train."

The game has ended and my dad says we should go have an early lunch. I suggest a small ethnic restaurant, what San Francisco is famous for. My father doesn't want to leave the area of Fisherman's Wharf. Scores of tourist restaurants are within walking distance of the motel. My dad prefers going to one of them.

On the way to the restaurant, my father recalls his visits to San Francisco when fishermen still came to Fisherman's Wharf. He acts as if I've never been here. I want to tell my father about the real San Francisco, where I've lived these past fifteen years. But he's only interested in the San Francisco of his travels, the city we flew out of on our way to Honolulu, where we ate fresh-cooked crab on Fisherman's Wharf and shivered in the legendary fog because, being tourists, we had worn our summer clothes.

When I was growing up, the places we lived looked like international bazaars of tourist junk. We had camel saddles from the Middle East, low lacquer tables from Japan and bamboo chairs from Hawaii including a queen's chair with a back that resembled an enormous fan. There were black wooden tiki gods the termites eventually devoured, a red Naugahyde and bamboo bar, large pieces of coral, aquamarine glass balls and fishing nets—all from the South Pacific. We even had a wooden lady, naked except for the lei around her neck, whose bare legs opened and closed to crack nuts.

It seemed perfectly normal to sit on a large red silk pillow on the floor, at a low lacquer table with an inlaid design of Mt. Fujiyama, to eat dinner and watch TV. It also seemed normal to eat the pseudo-international fare my mother whipped up from recipes she got at the officers' wives club, dishes we called "Chinese Chicken" and "Spanish Rice." It felt normal to live everywhere and nowhere and to think of life as an endless highway, with occasional stops for lunch and to buy souvenirs.

We have to walk slowly because my father is too frail to move at anything close to a normal pace. He doesn't pick up his feet when he walks. Instead, he slides one foot forward along the sidewalk and then slides the other one, as if he's using an invisible walker. He is bent over a bit and I find myself stealing glances at him to confirm that this frail old man is my dad.

My sister's husband never called my father by his name or by the more affectionate *Dad*. Instead, he referred to my dad as *The Commander*. The military title seemed apt for a man whose children felt like low-ranking members of his squadron.

Every Christmas during my childhood, my father directed the tree-trimming operation from his favorite olive-green chair next to the couch. Clutching a highball in his right hand, he would gesture at the tree with his left. The smoke from his cigarette, balanced on the edge of the ashtray, would cause lazy circles to rise in the air. Everything had to be done according to my father's specifications. Tinsel could never be clumped but had to be laid on a branch, one slippery silver strand at a time. The ornaments needed to be balanced, with the proper mix of large and small, and colors carefully chosen and carefully placed.

When I went anywhere on the base with my father, it was apparent who was in charge. Men snapped to attention whenever my father came near, their right hands flying to their foreheads like startled birds. My father appeared tall and proud then, his uniform smooth as a pressed and fitted sheet, his shoes shiny with reflective surfaces like mirrors. Airmen drove my father wherever he needed to go. Sergeants typed his letters. Nurses from his squadron babysat us kids.

After my father retired, he spent his days playing solitaire in front of the TV. Occasionally, he would look up from his cards to see what had come up on the screen. He lived from trip to trip, planning and talking about where he and his wife would go next and, afterward, reliving all the sights again and again. The world that had so much order and purpose, that my father once directed like a great chess master, could not be revived. All he could do with his old life was reminisce about it.

My father orders for me in the restaurant, as he always has. He shakes his head from side to side when the waiter asks if he would like a drink. My father, who could never be found without a cold beer or a highball or an extra-dry martini, is now a teetotaler. With all the drugs my father takes, the alcohol would kill him. He stopped smoking, as well, because of his heart and some problem with his lungs. He is no longer excessive and exuberant, the way he used to get after several drinks, the way I always remember him being.

I am afraid of this old man in a way that I was never afraid of his younger and stronger counterpart, though I was afraid of him, too. I am afraid because it feels as if someone has robbed my father of himself and left behind this shell who resembles my father but I know isn't really him. I spent my life trying to get my father's attention and approval and now it's too late. My father is on his way out. The guy I so desperately wanted to notice me has already left.

We shuffle back to the motel room and I know there isn't any point in staying. It's clear to me that I won't see my father again. I feel the way I do when I'm on the last page of a novel that kept my fierce attention for days and I see that it will come to a disappointing end.

I ask my father what time the train will be leaving and what time the train will be getting in. With nothing else to say, I gaze past my father's head, into the darkened room.

Suddenly, I picture my younger self, with wispy blond hair and a round face. The top of my head barely reaches my father's waist. I've got my right hand curled inside my dad's left. He's walking me across the base to get shots at the dispensary.

Moments later, the sharp sting of alcohol soaks the air and I feel it pressed cold and wet against my skin. "Keep looking at me, Shorty," my father warns, using the nickname he chose for me when I was young.

I turn and lock my gaze on a point of light emanating from my dad's brass belt buckle. He tightens his grip on my hand. Then I squeeze my eyes shut to steel myself against the pain.

"I guess I'll head off," I say. Holding onto the doorknob, my father leans over and plants his lips momentarily on my cheek.

I turn and watch my father close the door. The sunlight is a stark contrast to the darkness inside. For the first time, I notice that my hands are clenched into tight fists, my shoulders hunched close to my ears. I close my eyes, take a deep breath, and start to cry.

The last thing I want is to have my father step out and see me here bawling. I pull a Kleenex out of my bag, blow my nose, and dab my eyes. Whatever caused this sadness, I tell myself, isn't worth crying about.

As soon as I start walking, I see it out of the corner of my eye. The pool sits behind the semicircle of rooms, exactly where it's supposed to be. White plastic lounge chairs, empty now, face the water.

I step over to the grassy area that leads to the concrete. For a moment, I can almost smell the chlorine and feel the water caressing my skin.

Sunlight is rippling across the aquamarine oval like in a dream. I indulge myself with one last lingering look. The empty swimming pool sits waiting. As if I might be persuaded to dive back in.

B. E. Scully

Like Water and Stones

On the same day Jo turned thirteen, a girl drowned down by the lake. Summer vacation had just started and Jo didn't hear about it until everything was already over. The story had it that the girl fell out of a boat and didn't even try to swim to safety. She just disappeared beneath the water and wasn't seen again until the rescuers found her at the bottom. At least that's how the story had it.

After that the day of Jo's birth and the day of the girl's death were linked in her mind in some shared underwater world. Or maybe the link had always been there, right from the beginning. After all, she'd had an uneasy start in life, being named for something she wasn't. With two girls in the family already, her parents had tried one more time for a boy.

Mother's first words, faithfully preserved in Jo's pink baby book: "What is it?"

The father's first words went unrecorded.

They named her Jo, after her father Joseph, a compromise correction.

"Is that short for Joanne?" (or Josephine or Josie or even Jojo, as if she were a clown or small dog).

"No, just Jo," she would say.

So when Jo met Ray and all he said was, "Hey, Jo, nice to meet you," she decided right away to be on his side. Ray had been hired to teach martial arts at the local gym the same summer Jo turned thirteen and the girl drowned. Ray was somewhere within that wide and mysterious age range between Jo and her parents, but like a lot of things about Ray, nobody really knew for sure.

He had a deep and seemingly permanent tan—not the carefully monitored sun-screened kind, but the leathered sienna of road work and hard labor. Jo thought Ray might even have Asian blood in him. She liked to imagine him as an orphan in some mysterious, remote Chinese village, raised by black-belt monks until his true identity as the emperor's long-lost son forced him to go into hiding as a simple martial arts instructor in Blue River, Oregon.

Ray had come out of nowhere that summer, but the rumor was that he'd lost his previous job because of his drinking, not his secret identity.

"I'll tell you one thing," Bill Hanes down at the Quick Mart liked to say. "My cousin drives an ambulance down in Dorsey, and his team responded to a call where a car had run clear up onto the sidewalk. Driver was slumped over the wheel, dead out of it. Turns out it was our own Ray Shultz, believe it or not."

What everyone did believe was that drinking problem or not, Ray was one odd duck, always going on about the spirit world and unseen energies and that sort of New Age thing. But he also was one hell of a martial arts instructor, and they weren't half as easy to come by in Blue River, Oregon, as drunks.

Jo liked to be near the strange energy that vibrated outward from Ray like a live wire, electrifying and maybe a little dangerous, if you got too close. Just as electrifying was the way his body matched his personality—lean and sinewy, muscles wound like tight cords of rope. He had a habit of straining forward whenever he got excited, as if he were trying to burst out of his own skin and get ahead of himself somehow.

"The power of the mind—you wouldn't believe what you can accomplish with meditation alone," he'd tell her when she lingered around after class just to be near him.

"I believe it."

Ray laughed, but not in the way most adults did when talking to kids, as if they were making fun of them. "I'll bet you do. You're a believer from the word go."

Jo liked these conversations more than anything else in the world. Ray understood things that most of the people she knew had never even heard of. He also seemed to understand things about her that no one else did—not even her best friend Niki, who knew when she'd starting menstruating and what bra size she wore.

That summer Niki had gotten a boyfriend, and because she'd done it first she now sincerely wanted Jo to have one, too.

"Come with me and Andy bike riding this Thursday. He has a friend who is pretty cute."

"Can't. I have class with Ray on Thursdays."

"Ray, Ray, Ray, that's all you ever talk about. Maybe you should go out with Ray."

Jo tried to will the flush out of her cheeks, but Niki was too quick. "Oh, my God! You've got a crush on him!"

"No way!"

"You know what would be so funny? If you sent him an anonymous love letter. Like a 'Secret Admirer' type of thing!"

"No. Way. With double capitals and periods, Nik."

They eventually settled on a card with a sunset on the front and the line "You're so special to me" printed inside.

"You want to come off as mature," Niki advised her. "Interested, but not too interested."

They addressed it to the gym in care of Ray Shultz, and Jo's stomach twisted into a fist when the mailbox door swung shut. No getting it back now.

She had to wait two more excruciating days for Thursday. When the time finally came and Jo saw Ray standing at the door waiting for the yoga class before theirs to end, she almost turned around and ran home.

Mr. Burns was peering through the door at the class, mostly women, bending into downward-facing-dog. "You know one of the main differences between old women and young ones? The young ones' tits are way up here," he said, holding his hands high up against his chest, "and the old ones' tits are waaaaaay down here." He dropped his hands below his waist and swung them back and forth as if he had imaginary breasts flopping around like water balloons ready to break.

Jo pressed against the wall in an attempt to be invisible. They must not have seen her standing there—Mr. Burns, who had three kids of his own, would never have said that if he'd seen her standing there. The rest of the men, including Ray Shultz, never would have laughed.

But then Mr. Burns looked straight at her. "Tuck that away for a few more years, kid. Use 'em while you got 'em."

He winked and the other men laughed even louder. Jo didn't know if she was supposed to laugh along with them or not.

All through class, the card and Mr. Burns and the water balloons kept getting mixed up in Jo's mind. By the time Ray settled everyone into their cool-down meditation, she could hardly keep still. She opened one eye just a little, in order to watch him. He was moving around the room adjusting postures like always, and for the first time it occurred to her that maybe Ray hadn't even gotten the card. Maybe someone at the desk had opened it up by mistake and thrown it away. Jo felt a hand resting on top of her head, so light and quick that once it was gone, she wasn't sure it had been there at all. But when Ray told everyone to open their eyes, he was looking right at her. She knew that from then on, something new would be between them.

When Niki asked her about the card, Jo didn't hesitate. "Oh, he never said anything about it," she said, which actually wasn't a lie. "He probably never even got it."

For the rest of the summer Jo went to the mall and rode bikes with Niki and flirted with boys and hung around after martial arts class with Ray without one consideration of what this new something between them might be. But the martial arts club's annual Labor Day retreat at the campground by the lake considered it for her.

❖ ❖ ❖

The adults had the downstairs rooms and the kids were herded upstairs into open bunks, boys on one side, girls on the other. There were lots of little kids and teenagers running around, but nobody Jo's age. Her older sister Diane was glued to her boyfriend, and Ray was so busy getting everyone settled in that he hadn't even noticed she was there. By the time Jo got her soggy sandwich and apple for lunch, she was beginning to regret she'd even come.

The alcohol arrived after dinner. The women stayed inside drinking beer out of cans and cleaning up the dishes while the men went out back to drain the kegs, their loud bursts of laughter punctuating their wives' hushed conversation. The little kids were in bed and the teenagers had disappeared into the woods, and Jo wandered around feeling stupid and out of place until she discovered the front porch. It was dark and deserted—the perfect hiding place. She leaned against the back wall and looked at the stars, sleepy with dinner and the long trip. She had just started to doze off when the bang of the screen door brought her to her feet.

It was Mr. Burns, stumbling around in the dark. Jo thought about water balloons swinging waaaaaay down here, and pressed further into the shadows.

"Damn women tying up the bathroom all the time."

She Holds the Face of the World

She was just about to make her escape when the zip of his pants stopped her. He arched a stream of urine through the air and then staggered backwards, fumbling with his zipper.

"Hey, there, what are you doing out here in the dark all by yourself?"

"Just looking at the stars."

"Are you afraid to come out back with all of us wild men?"

Surprisingly quick, he put his hands against the wall, one on each side of Jo's head like flannel-shirt bars.

"How about a little kiss for a wild man, huh?"

His alcohol-fueled mouth moving toward hers set her in motion. With the timing of a slapstick comedy, Jo ducked under Mr. Burns' arms just as he leaned forward in a drunken kiss. At the same instant the screen door banged open a second time, and Mrs. Burns stepped out.

"What the hell is going on here?"

Even though Mr. Burns was still leaning with his hands against the now empty wall, Jo somehow understood that the question had been directed at her.

"Nothing. We were just . . . looking at the stars," she stammered. Even many years later she would marvel at how instinctively she had known to tell the lie.

"Get inside," Mrs. Burns told her husband. "You're drunk." She grabbed his arm and dragged him through the door without a backward glance.

Jo stayed on the porch for as long as she could stand the chilly night air and then ducked inside and up the stairs. She was almost to the top when Ray caught up with her.

"Hey, I've been looking for you." He was as drunk as Mr. Burns, holding onto the railing to steady himself. "I've been wanting to ask you—am I really?"

"Really what?"

"So special to you. The card. You sent it, right?"

He was grinning down at her, waiting for an answer he already knew. For a second Jo thought about denying it, just to see what he would say. But before she had a chance to answer one way or the other, he reached out and put his hand on top of her head the way he had done in class, and then ran his fingers down the side of her face, light as feathers. She felt something in her stomach go strange, but she forced herself to stay still. Just then loud, drunken voices drifted up the stairwell.

"How about a little midnight dip down at the lake?"

"You mean a little midnight skinny dipping?"

"Maybe the ghost of that dead girl will be floating around."

"Better bring along something stronger than beer then!"

"Hey, where's Ray? Ray! Where are you, man? We're going for a swim with a dead girl!"

Ray stood looking down at her in the shadowed light. Then he ruffled her hair like she was a little kid or a favorite pet and disappeared down the stairs without a backward glance.

❖   ❖   ❖

The next morning her sister Diane woke her up too early. "Did you sleep okay last night?"

"Pretty good."

"I thought I heard Ray up here," Diane said, forcing a laugh. "Was he trying to make a move on you or something?"

"Of course not! He was just saying goodnight, jeez!"

"Okay, well, whatever. Let's go get some breakfast. I'm starving."

Downstairs they joined the group of women gathered in the dining room drinking coffee. Diane settled into the last chair, leaving Jo the floor.

"I have to shave my legs every single day or else I'm like two sheets of sandpaper," one of the women was explaining. "It's such a pain."

"Definitely a pain," Diane joined in without missing a beat. "Men get off so lucky only having to worry about their faces."

"Men get off lucky in a lot of ways," another woman said.

The voice was hard and cold, and it took a second for Jo to realize that it had come from Mrs. Burns. When Jo looked up, Mrs. Burns was staring straight at her. "You might not understand what we're talking about, honey. Are you even old enough to have body hair yet?"

The naked hatred in her voice silenced the room. The women knew that the tribe had been disrupted, that some unspoken code had been broken. As if by some primal, equally unspoken understanding, they just as quickly concluded that Jo was to blame. Diane gave her a pitying look, but what could she do? Survival depends on the tribe.

Jo made herself invisible for as long as possible and then slipped out of the house. The men were out back passing an old rifle back and forth and shooting at empty beer cans. Ray saw her standing there and gave her a wink, but she turned away. Mr. Burns had seen her, too.

"Hey, Ray!" he shouted. "It's not safe with her out here and all these bullets flying around!"

"Go on back inside, Jo," Ray said, grinning and trying to catch her eye. "Only us overgrown boys are allowed to play cowboy."

But Jo didn't feel like grinning and she didn't feel like going back inside. She wandered into the woods and made her way down the path to the lake. Piles of crushed beer cans and empty bottles of booze littered the shoreline like evidence.

Jo walked to the end of the wooden pier and sat down. No one else was around. The water was a still, unbroken mirror. Jo thought about the girl down at the bottom of the lake. The morning air was damp and cold, but Jo suddenly stood up and stripped off her clothes. She stood there shivering in the mist rising off the water and then dove into the mirror, cracking its smooth perfection.

The ice-cold shock turned her limbs rigid and stiff, like a dead body. Jo let herself sink to the bottom where the drowned girl waited. When she didn't sink fast enough she pushed through the water and swam deeper into the silent underwater world.

She finally touched the sand and stones of the lake bottom. Her lungs were squeezed tight and her head seemed to be thumping in time to her heartbeat. A line of black began creeping into the edge of Jo's vision when she felt a solid something fill her hand—the bones of the drowned girl! But no, it was a stone, perfectly round and smooth apart from an oval-shaped groove on one side.

The blackness crept closer as the stone and the dead girl became mixed together in Jo's mind. The same water that had taken the girl had given the stone. It had come from the lake's rocky depths and been shaped by its currents. It had also shaped itself just by holding fast while every other stone and watery life form flowed past and collided with and slipped across its solid surface. And the stone had shaped all of those things in turn.

Jo laid her thumb in the oval-shaped groove. It fit perfectly, as seamless as if for thousands of years the water had been carving it especially for her. She tried it a few more times, taking her thumb out of the groove and putting it back—a perfect fit every time. She wrapped her hand around the stone's solid weight and kicked furiously until she broke the surface of the water. Keeping hold of the stone, Jo swam for the shore.

❖ ❖ ❖

Back at the campground everyone was settling down to lunch. Her sister was there waiting for her.

"Where have you been?" Diane demanded. "You didn't even help set the table! And why is your hair wet?"

Jo didn't bother with a lie this time. She reached into her pocket and there it was—the stone. It knew whether the girl had tried to swim to shore or just let the water take her. But the stone wasn't telling. Solid and silent, the stone didn't need to answer or even listen to the questions.

"You'd better get a seat before you end up having to sit on the ground," Diane said.

Jo started to search the table to see where Ray and Mr. Burns were sitting. Then she realized it didn't really matter anymore. It didn't even matter if she ended up sitting on the ground. Like the water, she could give and she could take; like the stone, she could shape herself even as she was shaped by others. She could keep her secrets or tell them; she could stay in the water or swim to shore.

Jo slid her thumb into the stone's perfect groove and smiled a secret, underwater smile.

Liza Langrall

Gene Kelly at the Door

Dear Evelyn:

I guess you're saying "I told you so" to those of us who thought you were a hypochondriac. Joyce-Ann called to say you passed away, just like that, on her kitchen floor, with a spoonful of apple butter in your hand. She thought perhaps you had choked, but apparently you hadn't even tasted it.

Wasn't it just last spring, when we were all having our age spots buffed at that hoity-toity spa, that Queenie suggested we predict our own deaths? It was a morbid suggestion then, almost unbearable to think about now. And you came up with that crazy idea about Gene Kelly ringing your doorbell and asking you to marry him. And Bill getting out his .22 revolver and aiming it at Gene Kelly's head, but between Bill's shaky hand and Gene's elegant dance evasion, the bullet ending up killing you. I guess death doesn't have quite the sense of humor you did.

I still have pictures of our spa weekend on my camera because Ron Jr. has yet to download them onto my computer. I clicked through them just now and had a good cry, although a few of them make me grin. There's one of the four of us in front of the fountain—me looking as old as dirt, probably from having to drive two hours in that awful rental car; Joyce-Ann squinting and hunching over, trying not to get sprayed by the water; Queenie kicking her leg out like a Rockette; and you with that serene smile of yours, like you vaguely recognize the photographer but you're not quite sure. What a foursome we made! I look at us and realize how much time has elapsed since college. None of us are the spring chickens we were back in '57. But then I think, Who wants to be young? I like myself better now.

You played a part in the woman I've become. All the hours you spent listening to me whine about my mother and marriage and kids—I ought to have written you a check for your counseling services. And that dark spell in my thirties when I thought that raising four boys was going to kill me—and I almost did myself the favor—I couldn't have made it through without you. I'll never forget the two days you lived at our house, feeding and dressing the children, ironing Ron's shirts, watering the plants, sweeping the outdoor carpet on the patio. At the end of those two days, you sat on the edge of my bed in your peach sweater set, and you said, "Get up Kitty. The sun is shining outside, and we're taking the boys to the park. Get up and put your lipstick on. You'll feel better with lipstick on. Dinner's in the oven, and we're going to get some fresh air." Oh, Evelyn, crazy as it sounds, I'd go back to that time in an instant if somehow it would keep you here.

The picture that means the most to me from the spa weekend is the one I snapped of you on our early morning walk down to the lake. Do you remember? Queenie wanted to sleep in, and Joyce-Ann said she was too fat for a hike, so you and I set out on our own. The whole forest was hushed with fog, remember? Then you spotted the blue heron in the water. The camera caught your face as you were turning toward me, forming the word "Look!" Your brown eyes are lit with a youthful glee. Your arm is lifting, pointing toward the water, and at the same instant the heron is raising its elegant, gray form into the air, its shoulders beginning to expand into flight. I took several more shots as it flapped gracefully above the trees, but the picture I come back to is the one of you, ahead of me on the trail, breathless over your discovery.

What will our Girls' Weekends become now? And that trip we were planning to Reno? You won't be there to defend Queenie's childish need for attention or Joyce-Ann's hideous crocheted sweaters. You won't scold us for staying up too late or entertain us with deadpan stories about Bill and his fingernail clippers or get that wilted look on your face when you catch sight of your rear end in the mirror.

You were always the peacemaker in our catfights—well, except for that one time at your daughter's wedding, but who can blame you? You were always the thoughtful, introspective one—had sense to keep your mouth shut more often than we did. Did you feel like the odd one out? You brought balance and stability to our zaniness. I'm not even sure what will happen to the three of us now. One of us will have to try to take your place as caretaker, speaker of reason.

Tomorrow's the big day. You know what I mean. I'm wearing that black dress you made me buy in Montreal. Joyce-Ann and Queenie are also wearing black, and to complete the ensemble we're all wearing the fruit-bowl earrings. Queenie begged the undertaker to put them in your ears, too, but he said those kinds of requests could only come through the family, and she didn't have the nerve to approach Bill about it. We will look horribly tacky, but we're doing it for you. You'll laugh when you see us, won't you? Take it as a symbol of our love.

When I start feeling guilty that I should have called you that morning, should have come over to your house and sat among your chrysanthemums, should have somehow kept you from going over to Joyce-Ann's to meet that fate—I have to stop and remind myself that we can't control the future. It would have happened whether you had been lying in a chaise longue or collecting your mail; it was just your time. I guess all those heart palpitations that we thought were ploys to get attention after your daughter's wedding were really signs of a weak heart. If I had known, I would have taken better care of you—all of us would. Joyce-Ann would have tried to force that congealed broth on you, and Queenie would have scrubbed the kitchen floor with one of your good washcloths, and I would have bored you to tears with stories of the grandkids.

Well, it's late. I'm not saying goodbye, just "I'll write more later." I'm going to go slice up a cucumber for my eyes to keep the swelling down. I'll miss you, dear friend.

If you see me anytime soon, you'll know that my prediction about the hot air balloon came true.

Always,
Kitty

Acknowledgments

Acknowledgments

All the poems and prose pieces in this anthology originally appeared in one of the following *VoiceCatcher* print anthologies or online in *VoiceCatcher: a journal of women's voices and visions* (www.voicecatcherjournal.org/archives.html).

VoiceCatcher 1:

"The Moth, the Last Night" by Amy Minato

"Starfish Time" by Jodie Buller

"Stoop" by Jennifer Springsteen

VoiceCatcher 2:

"After Finding Out My Sister's Pregnancy Is Not" by Shanna Germain

"Morning" by Miriam Feder

"Caring for Father" by Heidi Schulman Greenwald

"The Bösendorfer" by Alida Thacher

VoiceCatcher 3:

"Mama Takes a Bubble Bath" by Kristin Berger

"To Those Boarding Planes to Hawaii to Escape the Rain" by Judy Beaudette

"On the Book" by Oz Hopkins Koglin

"How Can You Live There?" by Bette Lynch Husted

"More Like Music" by Sage Cohen

"Sleep" by Emily Kendal Frey

"Solder" by Paulann Petersen

"Forget about Florence Nightingale" by Patricia Kullberg

"Quality Courts" by Patty Somlo

VoiceCatcher 4:

    "Rendezvous" by Rebecca Starks

    "Portrait of a Cowboy as a Young Girl" by Carolyn Martin

    "The Figurehead" by Darlene Pagán

    "Trucker's Atlas" by Favor Ellis

    "The Fujita Scale" by Toni Partington

    "Kali-Ma" by Amanda Sledz

    "Dying to Get Out of Here" by M

VoiceCatcher 5:

    "Osprey Circles" by Tiel Aisha Ansari

    "Birdsongs in Traffic" by Naomi Fast

    "I didn't keep it a secret, I just didn't tell you" by Celina Wigle

    "Pump House" by Marj Hogan

    "Vulvar Fantasy" by Nikki Schulak

    "Gene Kelly at the Door" by Liza Langrall

VoiceCatcher 6:

    "*nichos*: woman at the window" by Jodie Marion

    "The Amateur Tomato Breeder Flirts" by Jennifer Lesh Fleck

    "Guilt Poem: Conflict" by Brittney Corrigan

    "Three Rings at the Same Time and Performing Tigers" by Victoria Wyttenberg

    "Said & Meant II" by Meredith Stewart

    "Violet at the Creation" by Wendy Willis

    "Unexpected Conversation at Mid-Life" by Dawn Thompson

    "Some Shelter" by Kate Gray

    "Tango Club—Valparaiso" by Alice Hardesty

    "Robins" by Jill Elliott

"How I Learned to Rap in Jail" by Susan Russell

"This Morning" by Susan Dobrof

"30 Degrees from the Horizon" by Cara Holman

Fall 2012 Online Issue:

"Swan Song" by Jaime R. Wood

"We" by Carrie Padian

"Jailhouse Call" by Kelly Running

"315C" by Kristin Roedell

"spoon" by Brandi Katherine Herrera

"To the Friend Who Talked Me Down" by Amy Schutzer

"Running with Dragons" by Trista Cornelius

Winter 2013 Online Issue:

"The Old Life" by Andrea Hollander

"The Hundred Names of Love" by Annie Lighthart

"Decomposition" by Pat Phillips West

"Wisdom Tree" by Julie Rogers

Summer 2013 Online Issue:

"Three Facts about Sperm" by Ursula Whitcher

"Polaroid of My Mother" by Cindy Stewart-Rinier

"The Hand-Off" by Pattie Palmer-Baker

"Your Hand at Your Throat" by Karen Guth

"Black Sharpie" by Anne Gudger

Winter 2014 Online Issue:

"For a Hot Shot" by Susan DeFreitas

"Motherhood" by Elizabeth Stoessl

"Waiting for a Diagnosis" by Linda Strever

"Anticipation" by Penelope Scambly Schott

"Bridge" by Jennifer Liberts

"Messages" by Mary Mandeville

"Like Water and Stones" by B.E. Scully

Summer 2014 Online Issue:

"Thicker Than Water" by Claudia F. Savage

"Weddings I Have Ruined" by Tanya Jarvik

"Binders Full of Women" by Shawn Aveningo

"Aurelia Aurita: Moon Jelly" by Lois Rosen

"Still Life with Cabbage" by Margaret Chula

"A'ā" by Burky Achilles

"Relic" by Jennifer Foreman

"Talking Herself into Onward" by Melanie Green

"Carnage" by Heidi Beierle

"Tribes" by Thea Constantine

Winter 2015 Online Issue:

"Advice" by Donna Prinzmetal

"Two Poets in the Weight Room" by Tricia Knoll

"Under the sign of the water bearer" by Jennifer Kemnitz

"city spacious heart" by Pearl Waldorf

"A Passing Music" by Barbara LaMorticella

"Left As It Was, It Would Come Apart" by Jackie Shannon Hollis

"Ablaze" by Heather Durham

❖ ❖ ❖

Thank you to our hard-working anthology team:

Leslie Anderson, Prose reader
Mary Lou Anderson, Prose reader
Sara Bednark, Prose reader
Thea Constantine, Prose reader
Linda Ferguson, Prose reader
Stephanie Golisch, Prose reader
Allegra Heidelinde, Poetry reader
Christine Heise, Prose reader
Jennifer Kemnitz, Poetry reader
Leah Klass, Prose reader
Annie Lighthart, Poetry reader
Pattie Palmer-Baker, Poetry reader
Tammy Robacker, Poetry reader
Christi R. Suzanne, Prose reader

Shawn Aveningo, Designer

Shawn Aveningo is an award-winning, globally published poet whose work has appeared in over eighty literary journals and anthologies, including LA's *poeticdiversity*, who recently nominated her poetry for a Pushcart Prize. She is cofounder of The Poetry Box®, managing editor of the *Poeming Pigeon,* and online journal designer for *VoiceCatcher.* She is a proud mother of three who lives in Beaverton, Oregon, with her husband.

Meghana Mysore, Editorial intern and poetry reader

Meghana Mysore is a senior at Lake Oswego High School, where she gravitates toward all things word. She serves as a Portland Youth Poet Ambassador and has received several regional writing awards and recognitions. Besides words, she enjoys discovering and learning about new cultures and languages. She has been published in *Alexandria Quarterly, Burningword, Canvas, Crashtest, Eunoia Review* and more, and as a Young Voice in the Winter 2015 and Summer 2015 issues of *VoiceCatcher: a journal of women's voices & visions.*

Helen Sinoradzki, Copyeditor

Helen Sinoradzki has written a memoir, *Thursday's Child*, and published narrative nonfiction and short stories, most recently in *Crack the Spine*. An English teacher turned technical writer turned bookseller, she works at Powell's Books. She holds a PhD from the University of Illinois. A member of VoiceCatcher's board of directors, she was prose co-editor for the Winter 2015 and Summer 2015 online journal. She moved to Portland eighteen years ago and plans to stay for the rest of her life. Find her at helensinoradzki.com.

Nancy Flynn, Poetry Editor

Nancy Flynn grew up on the Susquehanna River in northeastern Pennsylvania, spent many years on a downtown creek in Ithaca, New York, and now lives near the mighty Columbia in Portland, Oregon. She attended Oberlin College, Cornell University, and has an English MA from SUNY Binghamton. She spent nearly two decades as a university administrator until she was liberated from the 9 to 5 in 2001. She was an assistant editor of *VoiceCatcher* 5 and an associate editor of *VoiceCatcher* 6, and her work appeared in *VoiceCatcher* 4 and the Summer 2015 online issue. A poetry collection, *Every Door Recklessly Ajar*, was published in 2015. More about her awards and publications is at www.nancyflynn.com.

Judith Pulman, Prose Editor

Judith Pulman writes in Portland, Oregon, where she also translates poetry from Russian, just to keep things light. Her work has been published in the *Los Angeles Review, Brevity Magazine, and Water~Stone Review*, as well as *VoiceCatcher* 6 and the Summer 2015 online issue. She received an MFA in 2012 from the Rainier Writing Workshop at Pacific Lutheran University, but edits and teaches writing all over. More of her writing is visible at www.judithpulman.com.

Tiah Lindner Raphael, Managing Editor

Although Tiah Lindner Raphael grew up amid the golden wheat fields of eastern Oregon, she now calls the greener hills of Portland, Oregon, home. A graduate of the master's program in book publishing at Portland State University, she is president of the VoiceCatcher board of directors 2015 and serves as ongoing managing editor for *VoiceCatcher: a journal of women's voices and visions*. Previously she served as both a prose co-editor and a poetry co-editor for the journal. Her work has been published in *CutBank* and *Paper Nautilus* among others.

Contributors

Artist and Writer Biographies

In addition to *VoiceCatcher*, **Alice Hardesty**'s poems have been published in various journals, such as *Fireweed*, *Verseweavers*, and the *West Wind Review*. Some have won awards from the Oregon Poetry Association. Her memoir, *An Uncommon Cancer Journey: The Cosmic Kick That Healed Our Lives*, about the radical healing of her husband from "terminal" cancer, was recently published by Bacho Press. In addition to writing, she loves neighborhood dog walks, chamber music, and good French food.

Alida Thacher is the cofounder of PDX Writers, which offers writing workshops, retreats, and editorial services. She is a certified facilitator in the Amherst Writers and Artists Method (AWA). She has published eight children's books, as well as several short stories and nonfiction pieces. She was an award-winning television producer and multimedia producer. She lives in Portland and is working on a young adult historical novel set in Portland in 1905.

Amanda Sledz is the author of *Psychopomp Volume One: Cracked Plate*. She is working on completing the second volume in the Psychopomp series, *All of Us Are Hiding*, and is polishing her debut science fiction novel, *The Falls Apart*. Read her philosophical ramblings, observations, and struggles to maintain the muse-writer relationship at amandasledz.com.

Amy Minato teaches reading and writing workshops in the Portland area, but considers the Wallowa Mountains her home. The possibilities latent in that open western landscape inspired "The Delivery." (She thanks the Pearls writing circle for their advice on this poem.) "The Moth, the Last Night" describes an actual experience—the almost spooky way nature has of reflecting our lives.

Amy Schutzer's second novel, *Spheres of Disturbance* (Arktoi Books/Red Hen Press, 2014), was chosen as a Finalist for an Oregon Book Award in 2015. Her first novel, *Undertow* (Calyx Books, 2000), was a Lambda Literary Award finalist, a Violet Quill Award finalist, and a Today's Librarian "Best of 2000" Award winner. She is the recipient of an Astraea Foundation Grant for Fiction and a grant from the Barbara Deming Memorial Fund. Finishing Line Press published *Taking the Scarecrows Down*, a chapbook of poetry, in 2011. She lives in Portland, Oregon, where she is hard at work on her next novel, and, as always, poetry.

Andrea Hollander's first full-length poetry collection received the Nicholas Roerich Poetry Prize; her fourth was a finalist for the Oregon Book Award. She is the recipient of two poetry fellowships from the National Endowment for the Arts, Pushcart Prizes in both poetry and nonfiction, and a poetry fellowship from Literary Arts of Portland, Oregon, where she has lived since 2011 and where she conducts writing workshops at both the Attic Institute and Mountain Writers Series.

Anne Gudger is a Portland writer, sometimes teacher, who noodles with words. She is grateful to have won second place in *Real Simple* magazine's 2013 Life Lessons essay contest, first place in the Willamette Writers 2013 Kay Snow Writing Contest, and third place in the *Writer's Digest* 84th Annual Writing Competition in 2015. She was a prose co-editor on the Winter 2014 issue of *VoiceCatcher: a journal of women's voices & visions*. She is working on a memoir on love and loss and how we get out of bed (and how we don't) while we grieve. She loves her two children and sweet husband.

Annie Lighthart started writing poetry after her first visit to an Oregon old-growth forest. Since those first strange days, she has published her poetry collection, *Iron String*, with Airlie Press; has had her poetry chosen by Naomi Shihab Nye to be placed in Ireland's Galway University Hospitals; and has had several poems read by Garrison Keillor on *The Writer's Almanac*. She has taught at Boston College, as a poet in the schools, and currently teaches workshops for Portland's Mountain Writers.

B.E. Scully lives in a round red house that lacks a foundation in the misty woods of Oregon with a variety of human and animal companions. She is the author of numerous novels, short stories, poems, and articles. Published work, interviews, and odd scribblings can be found at bescully.com. After discovering *VoiceCatcher* at a literary conference, she began submitting short stories and has been a fan ever since.

Barbara LaMorticella watches the clouds from a cabin in the hills outside Portland. She is a long-time poetry radio host. Her second collection of poems, *Rain on Waterless Mountain,* was a finalist for the Oregon Book Award. She was awarded the Holbrook Award for Outstanding Contributions to Oregon Literary Arts and the first Oregon Literary Arts Women Writers Fellowship. Retired from medical transcribing, she cares for her family, does radio, and works for social change.

Bette Lynch Husted sees the Columbia Gorge in all seasons in her monthly commute from eastern Oregon to her Portland-area "Side Porch Poets" writing group. In Pendleton, she coordinates the First Draft Writers' Series, watches birds, and practices T'ai Chi. Her books include two collections of memoir essays, *Above the Clearwater: Living on Stolen Land* (OSU Press) and *Lessons from the Borderlands* (Plain View Press), and the poetry collection *At This Distance* (Wordcraft of Oregon).

Brandi Katherine Herrera is a poet and multidisciplinary artist based in Portland, Oregon, whose recent work in poetic text, film, and sound has been performed for Poetry Press Week and Pure Surface, and featured in the *Common, Octopus Magazine, Poor Claudia,* the *Volta,* and *Word/For Word,* among others. A ltd. artist's edition of her experimental text + visual translations and poems, *Mutterfarbe,* using Goethe's *Zur Farbenlehre* as a primary source, is forthcoming from Broken Cloud Press.

Brittney Corrigan is the author of the poetry collection *Navigation* (The Habit of Rainy Nights Press, 2012) and the chapbook *40 Weeks* (Finishing Line Press, 2012). Her poems have appeared widely in journals and anthologies, and she is the poetry editor for the online journal *Hyperlexia: poetry and prose about the autism spectrum* (http://hyperlexiajournal.com). She lives in Portland, Oregon, where she is both an alumna and employee of Reed College. For more information, visit http://brittneycorrigan.com.

Burky Achilles began a spontaneous eruption of poetry in January of 2014 following the deaths of a good friend, her mother, and her mother-in-law in 2013. She also writes essays and creative nonfiction. Her essays have appeared in the *Chocolate for a Woman's Soul* series. She placed first in the poetry category at the 2015 Tucson Festival of Books Literary Awards. She was raised on Kauai and teaches high school English in Thailand. She was a poetry co-editor for the Winter 2015 issue of *VoiceCatcher: a journal of women's voices & visions.*

Cara Holman has called Portland home since 1991. While also writing and publishing personal essays, she feels most drawn to the Japanese poetry forms of haiku and haibun for expressing herself. Most recently, her poetry and prose have been featured in *Contemporary Haibun, Fear of Dancing, A New Resonance 9, Our Portland Story,* and *VoiceCatcher* 6. When not writing, Cara enjoys reading, gardening, practicing qigong, and teaching math and language arts to elementary school students.

Carolyn Martin is blissfully retired in Clackamas, Oregon, where she gardens, writes, and plays with creative friends. Her poems have appeared in publications such as *Antiphon, Naugatuck River Review, Persimmon Tree,* and *Stirring.* Her second collection, *The Way a Woman Knows,* was released in February 2015 by The Poetry Box®, Portland, Oregon. Carolyn served as president of VoiceCatcher from 2011–2014 and as the first managing editor of its online journal and website.

Carrie Padian is a person who is sometimes embarrassed by how intensely she feels things, but then she writes poems about them and that makes everything okay. Her work can be found in the online journals *Straight Forward Poetry* and the *Gravity of the Thing* as well as at carriepadian.com.

Celina Wigle (aka The Celestial Concubine) is an Oregon native and graduate of Portland State University. She was a poetry co-editor and recording engineer in 2012/13 for *VoiceCatcher: a journal of women's voices & visions.* She now lives in Manhattan, New York, developing herself as a Sexual Wellness Mentor, Postpartum/Full Spectrum Doula, and proud owner of Day One Doula: Manhattan. Her next adventure includes schooling to become a Postpartum Sex Therapist. She would like to remind you to live freely, poets are watching. www.CelinaWigle.com

Cindy Stewart-Rinier holds an MFA in Creative Writing from the Rainier Writing Workshop at Pacific Lutheran University, has served as a poetry co-editor for *VoiceCatcher: a journal of women's voices & visions* for three issues, and is an active member of Mountain Writers, for whom she teaches poetry workshops. Her work has appeared in *Ascent, Calyx, Crab Creek Review, Naugatuck River Review,* the *Smoking Poet,* and *VoiceCatcher,* as well as the anthology, *Siblings: Our First Macrocosm* (Wising Up Press). Four poems have been nominated for Pushcart Prizes.

Claudia F. Savage once cooked for people recovering from illness and wrote *The Last One Eaten: A Maligned Vegetable's History.* She has been published in *Bookslut,* the *Denver Quarterly, Nimrod,* and *Water-Stone Review;* teaches at the Attic Institute and through Savage Poetics; was a poetry co-editor for *VoiceCatcher: a journal of women's voices & visions;* wrote the series, "Leave the Dishes: Making Art While Raising Children," for the VoiceCatcher blog; is part of the poetry/music duo, Thick in the Throat, Honey; and has attended Ucross, Jentel, and the Atlantic Center for the Arts. Find her at www.claudiafsavage.com.

Darlene Pagán is the author of a chapbook of poems, *Blue Ghosts* (Finishing Line Press, 2011), and has published a full-length collection, *Setting the Fires*

(Airlie Press, 2015). Her poems and essays have appeared in many journals, including *Brevity, Calyx, Field Magazine, Hiram Poetry Review*, and *Literal Latté*, and have earned national awards and nominations for the Pushcart Prize and Best of the Net. She was an associate editor for *VoiceCatcher* 6 and a co-editor for the Summer 2013 and Winter 2014 issues of *VoiceCatcher: a journal of women's voices & visions*. She teaches at Pacific University in Forest Grove, Oregon.

Dawn Thompson oversees Portland Women Writers, which offers writing workshops focused on creativity, transformation, connection, and healing. She considers herself a space holder for women to build lasting pathways through the written word among their hearts, minds, bodies, and souls. Dawn spends as much time as possible with her son, Micha, and husband, Theo, in green spaces and is constantly tending her poetic heart.

Donna Prinzmetal is a poet, tutor, and psychotherapist. She has taught poetry and creative writing for more than twenty-five years to adults and children. Donna often uses writing to facilitate restoration and healing in her psychotherapy practice. Her poems have appeared in many journals including the *Comstock Review*, the *Journal*, and *Prairie Schooner*. Her first book, *Snow White, When No One Was Looking*, was published with CW Books in May of 2014. In 2014, she was youth editor for the Summer and Winter issues of *VoiceCatcher: a journal of women's voices & visions*.

Elizabeth Stoessl's poetry has appeared in two issues of *VoiceCatcher*. She is a transplant to Portland from the East Coast and a long career with the Arlington County, Virginia, Public Library. Her poems have been published in many journals, most recently *Blotterature, Measure*, and *Naugatuck River Review;* and in the anthologies *Creatures of Habitat* (Main Street Rag) and *Siblings: Our First Macrocosm* (Wising Up Press). She volunteers as a VoiceCatcher mentor.

Emily Kendal Frey lives in Portland, Oregon. She is the author of several chapbooks and chapbook collaborations, including *Frances, Airport, Baguette*, and *The New Planet*. *The Grief Performance*, her first full-length collection, won the Norma Farber First Book Award from The Poetry Society of America in 2012. Her second collection, *Sorrow Arrow*, was published in 2014 by Octopus Books and won the Oregon Book Award in 2015.

Favor Ellis grew up wild-eyed and wild deep on a small hill hidden in a forest. From the beginning, she practiced survival through story. She creates worlds, truthful and dark, peopled by the magical and small, the gorgeous and the grotesque. Small warm worlds that offer sanctuary from the loud fluorescent outside. She is making a home for herself in the Northeast Kingdom of Vermont, after living in Portland for many, many years.

Heather Durham is a naturalist and writer who is pursuing an MFA in creative nonfiction through the Northwest Institute of Literary Arts. Her essays have appeared in *Bacopa Literary Review, Pilgrimage Magazine,* and *Spry Literary Journal.* A city dweller with the soul of a hermit, she can often be found in the wild places in and around Portland with a journal, a field guide, and a pair of binoculars, head cocked and listening to the birds.

A resident of Portland, Oregon, **Heidi Beierle** works as a community planner, specializing in bicycle tourism and active travel options. Her creative work has appeared in *Alternatives, Herbivore, High Desert Journal, Journal for America's Byways,* and *VoiceCatcher.* She was nominated for a 2014 Pushcart Prize for her short essay, "Carnage."

Heidi Schulman Greenwald has published poems in a variety of journals and received awards from the Oregon Poetry Association. *Bear Deluxe* recognized her for excellence as an emerging poet writing about place. This past year, she began teaching creative writing to 5th through 8th graders. A member of *VoiceCatcher's* editorial collective, she served as a contributing editor of *VoiceCatcher* 2 and an assistant editor of *VoiceCatcher* 3 and 4. She lives with her husband and two children in Portland, Oregon, and can be found at heidigreenwald.com.

Jackie Shannon Hollis grew up on a ranch on the east side of Oregon, where the view was wheat fields, cattle, and combines. Now she lives in Portland where the view is cedars and raised-bed gardens. Her work has appeared in various literary magazines, including *Inkwell, Rosebud, Slice,* and the *Sun.* She has also contributed work to the online VoiceCatcher community. Her story here is part of her memoir. You can see more of her work at www.jackieshannonhollis. com.

Jaime R. Wood is the author of *Living Voices: Multicultural Poetry in the Middle School Classroom* (NCTE, 2006). Her poems have appeared in *DIAGRAM, Dislocate, Juked, Matter, Phantom Drift,* and *ZYZZYVA,* among others. She teaches literature, composition, and business writing at Clackamas Community College and lives in Portland, Oregon, in a 120-year-old house with her husband and their family of cats.

Jennifer Foreman is a loud-mouthed, fiery Texan who loves living in Portland. Her day job is socially worky stuff for the county. A local storyteller and poet, she is trying her hand at memoir. She has had several poems published and is now working on getting her prose published. She rides her bike "Sheshe" around Portland and adores her orange twin tabby cats in her spare time.

Jennifer Kemnitz lives and writes in Portland. She is a great defender of plant life and can be roused at any moment to an impassioned discussion of its innate intelligence. Her work has appeared in the *Kerf, VoiceCatcher*, and *We'Moon*, and has been anthologized by Poetry on the Lake and The Poetry Box. She is a reader for *We'Moon* and is proud to serve as a poetry co-editor for the Winter 2016 edition of *VoiceCatcher: a journal of women's voices & visions*.

Jennifer Lesh Fleck was born in San Bernardino, California, and has lived in and around Portland, Oregon, for over ten years. Her work has appeared in *Main Street Rag, McSweeney's, Xconnect*, and other places. She lives with her family in an old Dutch Colonial in downtown Vancouver, Washington.

Jennifer Liberts received degrees from California State University and Columbia University. She teaches English and works in an independent bookstore in Portland, Oregon, where she lives. Her work has appeared in *Narrative*, the *Paris Review, Subtropics, Switchback*, and *VoiceCatcher*.

Jennifer Springsteen is the cofounder of PDX Writers and a certified facilitator in the Amherst Writers and Artists method. She is the recipient of the 2008 Oregon Literary Arts Friends of the Lake Oswego Library William Stafford Fellowship for fiction, and a 2015 Fishtrap Conference Summer Fellow. Her stories have been nominated for two Pushcart Prizes. She was an assistant editor of *VoiceCatcher* 2, the associate editor of *VoiceCatcher* 3, and editor of *VoiceCatcher* 4. She completed her first novel, *American War Song*, and is at work on her second.

Born in England, **Jill Elliott** lived briefly in Holland and Germany, spent a twenty-five-year layover in Michigan, and was welcomed to Portland by double rainbows in 2005. She spends her days immersed in her organic garden and her novel. An assistant editor of *VoiceCatcher* 4 and 5, Jill was published in *VoiceCatcher* 3 and 6. Additional publications include creative nonfiction in *Ink-Filled Page*, the *Sun*, and *Where the Roses Smell the Best*.

Jodie Buller lives in the Skagit Valley, Washington. The poem "Starfish Time" came from a visit to Teddy Bear Cove on Chuckanut Drive. She manages a farmers market and a natural burial ground, and does event work for Subdued Stringband Jamboree and Death:OK.

Jodie Marion is from the Indian River region of Florida but has lived in the Pacific Northwest for the past sixteen years. She teaches writing and Spanish at Mt. Hood Community College. Recent poems have appeared in *Best New Poets 2011*, *Narrative* magazine, the *New Guard Literary Review*, and *VoiceCatcher*'s print and online journals. Her chapbook, *Another Exile on the 45th Parallel*, won the 2012 Floating Bridge Press Poetry Chapbook Award and was published that year. She lives in Vancouver, Washington, with her husband and four wild children. Her website is jodiemarion.com.

At one time, **Judy Beaudette** lived in Hawaii, where she taught high school math and English for three years—in near-perpetual sunshine. Recently, she returned to the Seattle area with her husband and daughter, where she writes for both businesses and nonprofits. Her favorite place to spend time—snow, rain, or shine—is the North Cascades, a mere two hours from her front door.

Julie Rogers is an artist, writer, science geek, and all around seeker resulting in many careers and having lived the world over. She has had two "Readers Write" pieces published in the *Sun* and is working on a full-length memoir. She is also working on a painting series depicting futuristic scenes related to long-term climate change. You can see more of her work at julesrogers.com.

Karen Guth is a writer and business consultant, as well as an advisor at Portland Community College's Small Business Development Center. Her writing draws from her background as an Iowa farm girl, wilderness guide, geologist, wife, mother, daughter, sister, avid reader, and student of human nature. She lives in Portland with her husband, Joe. They have a son and daughter, both in their twenties. She is at work on her first novel.

Kate Gray's first novel, *Carry the Sky* (Forest Avenue Press, 2014), attempts to stare at bullying without blinking. She is the author of three poetry collections and has also published essays. She is a teacher and writing coach. She and her partner live in a purple house in Portland, Oregon, with their sidekicks, Rafi and Wasco, two very patient dogs.

A native Oregonian and former teacher, **Kelly Running** passionately instills authenticity in her poetry and storytelling. Her poetry has appeared in the Fall 2012, Winter 2013, and Summer 2013 issues of *VoiceCatcher*'s online journal.

Medicine Wheel, the debut novel in her series, *The Lizzy O'Malley Mysteries*, was published in 2013. She works for a Portland nonprofit and is writing the second Lizzy O'Malley mystery, *Celtic Ties*.

Kristin Berger was a member of the *VoiceCatcher* editorial collective from 2011 to 2013, serving as co-editor for *VoiceCatcher* 6. She is the author of two chapbooks of poetry: *For the Willing* (Finishing Line Press, 2008) and *Changing Woman & Changing Man*: A High Desert Myth, forthcoming from persian pony press. She has received residencies from Playa, H. J. Andrews Forest/Spring Creek Project, and Starkey Experimental Forest and Range, and hosts poetry readings in her neighborhood, at the Lents International Farmers Market.

Kristin Roedell is the author of *Girls with Gardenias* (Flutter Press, 2013) and *Downriver* (Alrdrich Press, 2015). She has been nominated for Best of the Web and the Pushcart Prize. Her work has appeared in *Crab Creek Review*, the *Journal of American Medal Society, Switched on Gutenberg*, and *VoiceCatcher*. She was an assistant editor of *VoiceCatcher* 6.

Linda Strever is the author of *Against My Dreams* (poetry) and *Don't Look Away* (fiction). Her poetry has been published widely in journals and anthologies including *VoiceCatcher*. Winner of the Lois Cranston Memorial Poetry Prize, her work has been a finalist for numerous awards. She is a Pushcart Prize nominee and has an MFA from Brooklyn College.

Liza Langrall grew up on a diet of classic movies, so it is no wonder that Gene Kelly danced his way into one of her stories. While living in Beaverton, she attended a *VoiceCatcher* reading and left determined to add her own voice to the harmony of women she had heard. In 2010, Liza moved to the Shenandoah Valley, where she homeschools her two sons and successfully grows a garden of weeds each summer.

Lois Rosen has taught in Oregon, New York, Colombia, Japan, Costa Rica, and Ecuador. At Willamette University, she codirected the Advanced Institute of the Oregon Writing Project, was an Assistant Professor of English, and leads workshops for the Institute for Continued Learning. Her poetry books include *Pigeons* (Traprock Books, 2004) and *Nice and Loud* (Tebot Bach, 2015). The Rainier Writing Workshop granted her an MFA (2010). Published widely, both her fiction and poetry appear in *VoiceCatcher*.

M's work has appeared in a variety of journals and is anthologized in *The*

Widows' Handbook (Kent State University Press, 2014). Her chapbook, *To That Mythic Country Called Closure*, was released by Concrete Wolf Press in 2013. She was managing editor for the *VoiceCatcher* editorial collective and treasurer on the VoiceCatcher Board from 2009 to 2012.

Margaret Chula has been writing, teaching, and publishing Japanese-genre poetry for thirty-five years. Her seven collections include, most recently, *Just This*. She has been a featured speaker and workshop leader at writers' conferences throughout the United States, as well as in Poland, Canada, and Japan. In 2010, she was appointed poet laureate for Friends of Chamber Music and has served as president of the Tanka Society of America since 2011. Her current projects include a poetic memoir of living in Kyoto and a collection of lyrical poetry.

Marj Hogan is originally from Washington State and has spent the last eight years in North Portland, close to the river and trains. A Spanish teacher by profession and a writer by slow habit, she has published poems in *Bear Deluxe*, the *Charles River Journal*, the Cambridge, Massachusetts, *New Voices* series and *The Rendevous Reader: Northwest Writing*.

Mary Mandeville is a daughter, mother, sister, partner, friend. She derives sustenance from nature, from daring words onto the page, and from the company of people practicing the ferocious art of living well despite devastating loss. "Messages" was nominated for a Pushcart Prize; her essay "Zex" was featured in Portland's 2015 Listen To Your Mother; and her essay "Giant Sequoia" won Honorable Mention in the Hip Mama & Unchaste Readers Series Writing Contest.

Melanie Green is the author of two books of poetry, *Continuing Bridge* and *Determining Sky*. Both are available through Mountains & Rivers Press.

Meredith Stewart received an MFA in poetry from the University of Nevada, Las Vegas, in 2007. Her poetry has been published in *damselfly press, Ghost Town Poetry Anthology, Relief, Rock & Sling*, and the *Santa Clara Review*. She lives in Portland, Oregon, and teaches at Clark College and Warner Pacific College.

Miriam Feder writes with P-Town Playwrights and PDX Playwrights in Portland, Oregon. She produces PDX Playwrights' Fertile Ground Festival Productions (2013–2016). Each of these festivals has included a few of her short plays as well. She has produced the full-length plays *Ephemory* (2012) and *The Only Way Out is Through*, an original musical (2010). She is a member of the Dramatists Guild.

Miriam publishes original essays and more at http://miriamfeder.com.

Naomi Fast is the author of *Portland Light*, a collection of poetry and photography inspired by Portland. She was an assistant editor of *VoiceCatcher* 6, and her poetry and photography can be seen in *VoiceCatcher* 4 and 5. She is also locally published in the first *Ghost Town Poetry Anthology*, edited by Christopher Luna and Toni Partington. When not writing, Naomi is often heard singing to herself while out riding her bike. Her website is www.naomifast.com..

Nikki Schulak writes and performs comedy about bodies and relationships. Her first published work, "My Mid-life Thong Crisis," appeared in *VoiceCatcher* 3. "The Emperor's New Jump Rope" was an honorable mention in the 2012 Sports Poetry & Prose Contest. "On Not Seeing Whales" (Bellevue Literary Review) was chosen as a Notable Essay in *Best American Essays 2013*. She was an assistant editor of *VoiceCatcher* 6. She lives in Portland with her teenagers, her husband, her boyfriend, and her beloved dog, Calvin.

Oz Hopkins Koglin, a journalist turned poet, lives in Portland, Oregon. Her poems have appeared in *Hubbub*, the *Oregonian*, *Poetry Southeast*, and *VoiceCatcher*. She was a community organizer in St. Louis, Missouri, where she grew up, and was selected as a Danforth Foundation Metropolitan Fellow. She is a graduate of Reed College. In celebration of Oregon's sesquicentennial, *Poetry Northwest* and the Oregon State Library announced her chapbook, *Gardens For Everyone*, as one of the 150 outstanding poetry books of Oregon.

Pat Phillips West lives in Portland, Oregon. She has been nominated for a Pushcart Prize and Best of the Net. Her work has appeared in *Haunted Waters Press*, *Persimmon Tree*, *San Pedro River Review*, *Slipstream*, *VoiceCatcher*, and elsewhere. She previously wrote the VoiceCatcher blog's monthly prompt column.

Patricia Kullberg, MD, MPH, devoted her career to serving persons living with physical, mental, and addiction disorders at a clinic for the homeless. She has written many award-winning articles about health and medicine. Her novel, *Girl in the River*, was released in August 2015, by Bygone Era Books. Kullberg and her husband live in Portland, Oregon, where she facilitates writing workshops through Write Around Portland and volunteers at KBOO, a community radio station.

Pattie Palmer-Baker is a Portland, Oregon, artist and poet. Over the years of exhibiting her artwork—which combines collage and poetry in calligraphic form—she discovered that most people, despite what they may believe, do like poetry. She has been published in *Analekta, Eholi Gaduji Journal*, the *Ghazal Page, Martian Migraine Press, Petals in the Pan Anthology, Poeming Pigeons* and *Silver Press Blog*. VoiceCatcher nominated her for a Pushcart Prize in 2013, and she was a poetry co-editor for three issues of *VoiceCatcher: a journal of women's voices & visions*. Her website is www.pattiepalmerbaker.com.

A member of the editorial collective for *VoiceCatcher* 3, **Patty Somlo** had essays in *VoiceCatcher* 1 and 3. She has received four Pushcart Prize nominations, been nominated for storySouth's Million Writers Award and had a piece selected as a Notable Essay for *Best American Essays 2014*. Her forthcoming books are *Even When Trapped Behind Clouds* (WiDo Publishing), a memoir in essays that includes pieces published in *VoiceCatcher*, and *Hairway to Heaven Stories* (Cherry Castle Publishing).

Paulann Petersen, Oregon Poet Laureate Emerita, has six full-length books of poetry, most recently *Understory*, from Lost Horse Press in 2013. Her poems have appeared in many journals and anthologies, including *Calyx*, the *New Republic, Poetry, Prairie Schooner, Willow Springs*, and the Internet's *Poetry Daily*. She was a Stegner Fellow at Stanford University. A friend of VoiceCatcher founder Diane English, she was an early and ardent supporter of the VoiceCatcher vision.

Pearl Waldorf divides her days between her hard-earned right livelihood as a body-centered psychotherapist and the sweet home she shares with her partner (and her partner's dog) in North Portland. Between good friends, shared meals, and the richness of urban living (not to mention emails, exercise . . .), she's not sure where she finds the time to write. She was an assistant editor of both *VoiceCatcher* 2 and 3. A shout out: Professional artists, you work your asses off to make our world more beautiful. Thank you.

Penelope Scambly Schott is a past winner of the Oregon Book Award for Poetry for her verse biography *A Is for Anne: Mistress Hutchinson Disturbs the Commonwealth*. Her newest book is *How I Became an Historian*. She lives in Portland and Dufur, Oregon, where she teaches an annual poetry workshop. The workshop topic this year was *Surprise!*

Rebecca Starks' poems have appeared in the *Carolina Quarterly, Crab Orchard Review, Poetry Northwest, Slice*, and elsewhere. Her short story "Roman Road," a finalist for the 2015 Jack Dyer Fiction Prize, appeared in *Crab Orchard Review*.

She edits *Mud Season Review* and teaches lifelong learners at the University of Vermont.

Sage Cohen is the author of *Writing the Life Poetic*, *The Productive Writer*, and *Fierce on the Page* (forthcoming), all from Writer's Digest Books, and the poetry collection *Like the Heart, the World* from Queen of Wands Press. She served as poetry editor for *VoiceCatcher* 4, and her poems have appeared in *VoiceCatcher* 2, 3, and 5. She offers strategies and support for writers at pathofpossibility.com and for divorcing parents at radicaldivorce.com.

Sarah Fagan is a native New Englander who received a BA in Fine Arts and English Literature in Boston. She worked as an editor for a New England arts magazine before relocating to Portland, Oregon, in 2009. There she concentrated on her own art making, attending a post-baccalaureate program at the Oregon College of Art and Craft. Today she is primarily a painter, represented in Portland by Blackfish Gallery and various galleries across the U.S. Sarah is spending 2016 at an artist residency in Concord, Massachusetts.

Shanna Germain claims the titles of leximaven, vorpal blonde, and Schrödinger's brat. Her award-winning poems, essays, short stories, articles, games, and books have been widely published and she is the co-owner of Monte Cook Games. Her most recent books include *The Lure of Dangerous Women* and *As Kinky As You Wanna Be*. Visit her wild world of words at www.shannagermain.com.

Shawn Aveningo is an award-winning, globally published poet whose work has appeared in over eighty literary journals and anthologies, including LA's *poeticdiversity*, who recently nominated her poetry for a Pushcart Prize. She is cofounder of The Poetry Box®, managing editor of the *Poeming Pigeon*, and online journal designer for *VoiceCatcher*. She is a proud mother of three and lives in Beaverton, Oregon, with her husband.

Susan DeFreitas is a writer, editor, and spoken word artist. Her fiction, nonfiction, and poetry have appeared in *Fourth River*, the *Nervous Breakdown*, *Southwestern American Literature*, *Story Magazine*, *Utne Reader*, and *Weber—The Contemporary West*, among other publications, and in 2014 her work was a finalist for a Best of the Net award. She is the author of the fiction chapbook *Pyrophitic* (ELJ Publications) and holds an MFA from Pacific University. She lives in Portland, Oregon, where she serves as an editor with Indigo Editing & Publications.

Susan Dobrof is a retired labor and employment lawyer who lives in Portland,

Oregon. Now she studies and teaches yoga and studies and practices meditation; these life changes have allowed her to fully experience the joy of walking around the block with her cat. She has been published in the online journal *Halfway Down the Stairs* and *Momentum,* the magazine of the National Multiple Sclerosis Society.

Susan Russell is a criminal defense attorney now working as a public defender in Portland, Oregon. An eternal student, she enjoys classes about cooking and food as well as apparel design. Her other interests include gardening and car maintenance—a must for someone who drives her father's 1952 MG. When not busy chasing her dreams, Susan likes to taste wine, eat chocolate, and travel abroad. She does volunteer work for several organizations including Write Around Portland, where she has facilitated workshops.

Ever since she could put a pen (read: crayon) to paper, **Tanya Jarvik** has been an avid wordwanderer. She has taught composition, poetry, fiction, and memoir writing, and is a freelance editor and live storyteller. Tanya's work has appeared in the *Enter at Your Own Risk* anthology series, the *Manifest Station, VoiceCatcher,* the *Open Face Sandwich,* and elsewhere. One of her favorite gigs is writing a pseudonymous advice column for people in alternative relationships.

Thea Constantine was born in New York City into a family of actors and writers. She grew up in Hollywood, spent her youth in the clubs and streets of Los Angeles, and finally settled in Portland, Oregon. She is certified as an Amherst Writers and Artists facilitator and teaches weekly workshops with PDX Writers. Recent short stories have appeared in *In Focus* magazine, *Roving Writers, Stellazine,* and *Watercress Journal.* Her forthcoming book, *Stumptown,* began as a serial for the online magazine, the *Black Boot.* She co-wrote VoiceCatcher's monthly prompt column from 2013 to 2015 and looks forward to working as a prose co-editor for VoiceCatcher's journal in 2016. More at www.theaconstantine.com.

Tiel Aisha Ansari is a Sufi and data analyst living in the Pacific Northwest. Her work has appeared in *Fault Lines, Mascara, Measure, Verseweavers, Windfall,* and an *Everyman's Library* anthology, among others. Her poetry has been featured on KBOO, *Prairie Home Companion,* and MiPoRadio. Her collection, *Knocking from Inside,* is from Ecstatic Exchange, and her chapbook, *High-Voltage Lines,* is from Barefoot Muse. She serves as president of the Oregon Poetry Association. Visit her online at knockingfrominside.blogspot.com

Toni Partington lives and works as a poet, visual artist, and life coach in Vancouver, Washington. She is the cofounder with Christopher Luna of Printed Matter Vancouver, a small press focused on poetry; since 2004, they've hosted the Ghost Town Poetry Open Mic, now at the Angst Gallery. She is the author of two poetry volumes, *Jesus Is a Gas* (2009) and *Wind Wing* (2010). She was an associate editor of *VoiceCatcher* 5 and co-editor of *VoiceCatcher* 6.

Tricia Knoll is a Portland, Oregon, poet who adores VoiceCatcher for its role in providing inspiration, publication, and readings for regional writers. She has served in the VoiceCatcher mentor program. Her poetry has appeared in dozens of regional, national, and international journals or anthologies. Her chapbook, *Urban Wild*, is out from Finishing Line Press. *Ocean's Laughter*, poetry about the north Oregon coast, comes out from Aldrich Press in late 2015. Her website is triciaknoll.com.

Trista Cornelius taught college English for fifteen years and now writes and illustrates Storybooks You Can Color, the kind of coloring books she wanted as a kid: engaging stories and compelling characters that you get to color yourself. You can see her work at carrotcondo.com and read about her efforts to lead a creative life at allbutthekitchensink.wordpress.com. Trista also wrote VoiceCatcher's writing column *Dotting Your Ts and Crossing Your Eyes*.

Ursula Whitcher grew up in West Linn, Oregon, where she learned to drive on twisty roads and distinguish types of mist. She is employed as a mathematician at a university located in a former logging town in the old Northwest.

Victoria Wyttenberg grew up in Southern Oregon and has lived in Portland, Oregon, since 1970. She holds an MFA from the University of Washington and taught high school for many years. She has published poems in *Alaska Quarterly Review, Calyx, Clackamas Literary Review, Malahat Review, Poetry Northwest,* and other journals and anthologies. She is also an art student with particular interest in drawing and painting the figure. The circus remains a favorite metaphor for her since, like life, it can be confusing, scary, funny, beautiful, and sad; has many things happening at once; and has some very real dangers.

Wendy Willis is a poet and essayist. Her first book of poems, *Blood Sisters of the Republic*, was released in 2012 by Press 53. Wendy is also the Executive Director of Kitchen Table Democracy. Though she is originally from Lane County, she now lives in Portland with her family.

Index of Contributing Writers

Achilles, Burky: 80

Ansari, Tiel Aisha: 22

Aveningo, Shawn: 41

Beaudette, Judy: 63

Beierle, Heidi: 139

Berger, Kristin: 28

Buller, Jodie: 45

Chula, Margaret: 50

Cohen, Sage: 85

Constantine, Thea: 176

Cornelius, Trista: 135

Corrigan, Brittney: 29

DeFreitas, Susan: 14

Dobrof, Susan: 156

Durham, Heather: 195

Elliott, Jill: 99

Ellis, Favor: 72

Fast, Naomi: 23

Feder, Miriam: 75

Fleck, Jennifer Lesh: 12

Foreman, Jennifer: 89

Frey, Emily Kendal: 90

Germain, Shanna: 26

Gray, Kate: 66

Green, Melanie: 93

Greenwald, Heidi Schulman: 79

Gudger, Anne: 158

Guth, Karen: 147

Hardesty, Alice: 83

Herrera, Brandi Katherine: 68

Hogan, Marj: 76

Hollander, Andrea: 37

Hollis, Jackie Shannon: 142

Holman, Cara: 166

Husted, Bette Lynch: 65

Jarvik, Tanya: 19

Kemnitz, Jennifer: 48

Knoll, Tricia: 15

Koglin, Oz Hopkins: 64

Kullberg, Patricia: 107

LaMorticella, Barbara: 91

Langrall, Liza: 212

Liberts, Jennifer: 82

Lighthart, Annie: 59

M: 149

Mandeville, Mary: 180

Marion, Jodie: 10

Martin, Carolyn: 36

Minato, Amy: 11

Padian, Carrie: 27

Pagán, Darlene: 42

Palmer-Baker, Pattie: 51

Partington, Toni: 86

Petersen, Paulann: 92

Prinzmetal, Donna: 9

Roedell, Kristin: 39

Rogers, Julie: 130

Rosen, Lois: 43

Running, Kelly: 32

Russell, Susan: 120

Savage, Claudia F.: 17

Schott, Penelope Scambly: 77

Schulak, Nikki: 187

Schutzer, Amy: 88

Scully, B.E.: 204

Sledz, Amanda: 118

Somlo, Patty: 197

Springsteen, Jennifer: 105

Starks, Rebecca: 16

Stewart, Meredith: 56

Stewart-Rinier, Cindy: 49

Stoessl, Elizabeth: 33

Strever, Linda: 38

Thacher, Alida: 167

Thompson, Dawn: 61

Waldorf, Pearl: 67

West, Pat Phillips: 78

Whitcher, Ursula: 25

Wigle, Celina: 24

Willis, Wendy: 58

Wood, Jaime R.: 20

Wyttenberg, Victoria: 53

About VoiceCatcher

VoiceCatcher is a nonprofit community that connects, inspires and empowers women writers and artists in the greater Portland, Oregon/Vancouver, Washington. area in a variety of ways including:

> Publishing *VoiceCatcher: a journal of women's voices & visions*, our semi-annual online journal, which showcases the best writing and artwork by women in our area.
>
> Sponsoring events such as readings and art exhibits to celebrate the contributors of each journal.
>
> Providing an online community for women to share their successes, collaborate with other artists and writers, and publish articles related to the craft of writing or essays on living the creative and artistic life.
>
> Engaging some of the finest teachers in the area to present a series of fundraising workshops on the art and craft of writing and visual art.
>
> Collaborating with other literary and arts organizations to join forces in strengthening the voice of women.
>
> Expanding our social media outreach to grow the VoiceCatcher community and attract future generations of women writers and artists.

VoiceCatcher started as, and remains, an all-volunteer organization. That means its vision only becomes reality when women who share the dream step up to help. If you feel called to join the current community of VoiceCatcher in any capacity, please let us know by emailing us at info@voicecatcher.org or visiting the "make contact" page on our website: www.voicecatcher.org.

We've only just begun to find new creative ways to further the pioneering work of VoiceCatcher's founders. We thank them for their vision and hope you will find ways to lend your voice to ours. Together, we are all poised to achieve greatness.

A member of the Oregon Cultural Trust, VoiceCatcher is a 501 (c)(3) non-profit organization.

www.VoiceCatcher.org

www.VoiceCatcherJournal.org

www.Facebook.com/VoiceCatcher/